Increase Online Sales Through

Viral Social Networking

How to Build Your Website Traffic and Online Sales Using Facebook, Twitter, and LinkedIn —

In Just 15 Steps

STEPHEN WOESSNER

Increase Online Sales Through Viral Social Networking: How to Build Your Website Traffic and Online Sales Using Facebook, Twitter, and LinkedIn — In Just 15 Steps

Copyright © 2011 Stephen Woessner

1405 SW 6th Ave. • Ocala, Florida 34471 • 800-814-1132 • 352-622-1875–Fax
Web site: www.atlantic-pub.com • E-mail: sales@atlantic-pub.com

SAN Number: 268-1250

Woessner, Stephen, 1972-
  Increase online sales through viral social networking : how to build your web site traffic and online sales using Facebook, Twitter, and Linkedin--in just 15 steps / by Stephen Woessner.
      p. cm.
  Includes bibliographical references and index.
  ISBN-13: 978-1-60138-316-7 (alk. paper)
  ISBN-10: 1-60138-316-9 (alk. paper)
  1. Internet marketing. 2. Online social networks--Economic aspects. 3. Social media--Economics aspects. 4. Selling. I. Title.
  HF5415.1265.W63 2011
  658.8'72--dc22

                               2011002157

PROJECT MANAGER: Melissa Peterson • mpeterson@atlantic-pub.com
BOOK PRODUCTION DESIGN: T.L. Price • design@tlpricefreelance.com
PROOFREADER: Brett Daly • brett.daly1@gmail.com
FRONT COVER DESIGN: Meg Buchner • megadesn@mchsi.com
BACK COVER DESIGN: Jackie Miller • millerjackiej@gmail.com

Printed in the United States

Printed on Recycled Paper

We recently lost our beloved pet "Bear," who was not only our best and dearest friend but also the "Vice President of Sunshine" here at Atlantic Publishing. He did not receive a salary but worked tirelessly 24 hours a day to please his parents. Bear was a rescue dog that turned around and showered myself, my wife, Sherri, his grandparents  Jean, Bob, and Nancy, and every person and animal he met (maybe not rabbits) with friendship and love. He made a lot of people smile every day.

We wanted you to know that a portion of the profits of this book will be donated to The Humane Society of the United States. *–Douglas & Sherri Brown*

The human-animal bond is as old as human history. We cherish our animal companions for their unconditional affection and acceptance. We feel a thrill when we glimpse wild creatures in their natural habitat or in our own backyard.

Unfortunately, the human-animal bond has at times been weakened. Humans have exploited some animal species to the point of extinction.

The Humane Society of the United States makes a difference in the lives of animals here at home and worldwide. The HSUS is dedicated to creating a world where our relationship with animals is guided by compassion. We seek a truly humane society in which animals are respected for their intrinsic value, and where the human-animal bond is strong.

Want to help animals? We have plenty of suggestions. Adopt a pet from a local shelter, join The Humane Society and be a part of our work to help companion animals and wildlife. You will be funding our educational, legislative, investigative and outreach projects in the U.S. and across the globe.

Or perhaps you'd like to make a memorial donation in honor of a pet, friend or relative? You can through our Kindred Spirits program. And if you'd like to contribute in a more structured way, our Planned Giving Office has suggestions about estate planning, annuities, and even gifts of stock that avoid capital gains taxes.

Maybe you have land that you would like to preserve as a lasting habitat for wildlife. Our Wildlife Land Trust can help you. Perhaps the land you want to share is a backyard—that's enough. Our Urban Wildlife Sanctuary Program will show you how to create a habitat for your wild neighbors.

So you see, it's easy to help animals. And The HSUS is here to help.

2100 L Street NW • Washington, DC 20037 • 202-452-1100
www.hsus.org

TRADEMARK DISCALIMER

DEDICATION

I dedicated my first book to my wife, daughter, mother, and some of my closest friends who have shared their love and encouragement with me. It was their support that made me believe that I could actually write a book. This still feels like a dream I began living in March 2009. But, if this is a dream, I do not ever want to wake up!

So, I am taking this opportunity to thank some additional members of my tremendous family. Without their support, love, and guidance, these books would not have been possible because I would likely not be here to write them.

To my Aunt Elaine and Uncle Bill: I ate more meals at your house than at my own, and you always treated me like a son. Aunt Elaine, I love how to this day, you still call me "Stevie Boy." My heart melts every time. Uncle Bill, I still remember how I spent weekends at your house with all my cousins. I remember all of the Cleveland Indians baseball games you took me to, as well as banging pots and pans on New Year's Eve while standing on your front porch. You and Aunt Elaine included me in everything, and I love you so much for that. Thank you!

My life growing up was truly like the movie *My Big Fat Greek Wedding*. My family is so important to me, and we spent tons of time together. And because of that, my cousins are like my brothers and sisters. Thanks Dean, Stephanie, Peter, Maria, and Anthony. I miss you all so much!

To my Aunt Chris and Uncle Bill (yes, I have two Uncle Bills): I will never forget all of the summer pool parties in your backyard and the hospitality you showed everyone. Uncle Bill, thanks for instilling in me a strong work ethic that I still practice to this day. You are my godfather, you are my friend, and you taught me many life lessons. Not to mention, you make the best gyros and rice pudding ever! When are you and Aunt Chris going to start delivering to Wisconsin? Aunt Chris, you are my godmother and the quiet glue that binds our family together. Your loving nature is a special gift that you generously share with all of those around you. You are a role model for all of us to follow.

To my Uncle Mark and Aunt Cindy: I appreciate all of the time we spent together at grandma and grandpa's house cooking out and reminiscing about old stories. Uncle Mark, thanks for teaching me how to develop confidence, be strong, and be relentless while starring into the face of adversity. I appreciate all of the time we spent together on the golf course, especially the round we played several days before I left for Air Force basic training. Aunt Cindy, you have always been the caring spirit in our family. You maintained the calm through good times and through challenging times. You, Uncle Mark, Hilary, and Erika always made me feel special, valued, and important. I will never forget that!

I remember everything about growing up in North Canton, Ohio. I love going home, and I treasure all of the special memories. I look forward to making more. You all had a hand in shaping who I am today. From the bottom of my heart, thank you for everything. I love you all very much!

I would also like to thank Douglas Brown for giving me the opportunity to write a second book for Atlantic Publishing. I was a first-time author when I wrote *The Small Business Owner's Handbook to Search Engine Optimization*. Doug, you took a risk on my first book, and I appreciate it very much. Thank you for believing in me and becoming a trusted mentor.

TABLE OF CONTENTS

Chapter 3: Twitter Fundamentals 61

Chapter 4: LinkedIn Fundamentals 87

Chapter 5: Building Your Online Community 123

Chapter 6: Give Your Community Members What They Want – Great Content..165

PREFACE

I love seeking out challenges that push me to be better and to reach new levels I did not think I could reach. I literally thought I had met my match on a crisp, early morning in April 2000 when I successfully climbed Mt. Hood. It was on that day that I learned the keys to total happiness. I learned that my ability to focus and relentlessly pursue what I loved and wanted most in this world were the keys to making me happy. On that April morning, there were times I definitely felt like quitting and giving up the pursuit, but I did not give in — and I am so glad that I pushed forward because total happiness found me that morning on the side of Mt. Hood.

I had arrived in Portland, Oregon, several days earlier to continue the due diligence process regarding a company called Global Health & Fitness (GHF). Chad and Jody Tackett owned the company, and it represented a very strategic acquisition for the company I had recently founded called FortifiedNutrition.com (FN). From the moment I landed, Chad Tackett and I worked well together and got along great. Our personalities and goals were completely in sync. A friendship that lasts to this day had been born.

The idea for climbing Mt. Hood came up after Chad and I had finished playing basketball with some of his friends and eating too much pizza one night. While we stood around the kitchen, one of Chad's friends asked him what we planned to do the next day, and at that point, there was nothing on the agenda. So, when Chad suggested we climb Mt. Hood, it sounded like a once in a lifetime opportunity. I had no idea what I had just agreed to do, but I would quickly find out.

I woke up early the next morning with a nervous and anxious feeling in the pit of my stomach. Was I seriously going to attempt the climb? How had I let Chad talk me into it this? I was starting to reconsider the wisdom of my decision for several important reasons.

First, Mt. Hood is the highest mountain in Oregon and the fourth highest in the Cascades. It is approximately 11,200 feet high and home to 12 glaciers. Mt. Hood is also considered to be the most likely volcano in Oregon to erupt — super.

Second, Chad was in significantly better cardiovascular condition than I was. Consequently, I was afraid of being left in the snow only to be found in late May by some unsuspecting skiers. My body had been trained for lifting heavy objects and moving them from point A to point B — not snowshoeing up the side of a mountain — so my endurance would likely be a problem.

Third, I had never been snowshoeing, and physical coordination is not one of my strengths. In fact, our family doctor laughs at me each time I get a physical because I have zero reflexes. And lastly, as if there needed to be any additional reasons to cancel, I lacked the experience of doing anything physical in high altitude, which meant that my energy level would be a real and present issue.

There I sat in the hotel lobby waiting for Chad to pick me up. I tried to choke down a protein bar while my stomach continued to churn, and then it was time. Chad drove up, and we were off to get our gear at the nearby outfitter. Trying on the snowshoes was almost laughable because I wear a size 12 shoe so the snowshoes I received were enormous. The footprint the shoes left in the snow made it look like Sasquatch was out on the mountain that day. Plus, the ridiculous size of the snowshoes decreased the mediocre amount of dexterity that I possess.

Then, we packed up all of our gear, which consisted of snowshoes, boots, and some ski poles. I thought to myself, "Hey, how about some food and water?" I did not realize that this was just going to be an extended cardio session for Chad, but it would physically push me to the edge. As we pulled up to the base of the West Leg Trail, I could see a collection of skiers who had just finished their decent from Mt. Hood. The West Leg Trail is one of Mt. Hood's most popular ski trails that curves and twists its way from Timberline Lodge down the southern flank to the base of the mountain. All totaled, the trail is 5.5 miles long. Our plan was to climb up the trail until we reached the lodge, which is located just below Palmer Glacier. In addition to the somewhat daunting length of the trail, Chad and I would be climbing a significant incline and covering about 5,000 feet in elevation. Our goal was to complete the climb in approximately three hours so we could have lunch at the lodge. It all sounded like a good plan, but I was naïve.

We got out of the truck and organized our gear. I snapped on my snowshoes and grabbed the ski poles. I put on my sunglasses, took a deep breath, and exhaled. "You can do this," I chanted to myself. I hoped that the sweatshirt, T-shirt, and jeans I was wearing would be sufficient for the climb. I had no idea what I should be wearing. Chad looked at me and smiled. He could see from the anxious expression on my face that I was nervous and had no idea what to expect. Chad said something to me that I suspect was supposed to instill some level of confidence and encouragement, but all I heard was mumbling. I had tuned everything out and was trying to focus.

And then we were off. I looked ahead as far as I could follow the trail. It ascended and then headed into a tree line. The sun's glare reflecting off the snow was nearly blinding. It was one of the most impressive and beautiful scenes I have ever witnessed. Just being in the presence of all that grandeur was incredibly awe-inspiring.

That captivated feeling quickly faded during the first ten minutes of the climb because I thought my heart was going to leap out of my chest. Granted, I already had assumed that my lack of conditioning would be an issue, but I never imagined that I would begin feeling the effects in such a short time. I thought I might have a heart attack and die right there at the base of Mt. Hood — and it was only going to get worse.

Chad saw that I was struggling so he coached me on how to develop a rhythm with the snowshoes and poles. "And do not forget to breathe," Chad said to me. "Gee, thanks for the pearl of wisdom," I thought sarcastically to myself.

"And how can we be inclining already? Doesn't this mountain come with some sort of test trail or something so we can properly warm up? Come on!"

Once I focused on following Chad's sequential process of pulling, stepping, and breathing my way up the trail, my efforts became more efficient and effective, and I covered more ground using less energy, which are all good things. I am convinced that Chad was enjoying the thoughts of the physical torture that the trail was about to inflict on me.

As we continued our ascent, my mind began to wander to many things that had nothing to do with the climb. The fatigue and thinning oxygen levels were setting in and causing me to lose my focus. Chad could see I had begun to mentally wander so he started chatting with me and asking all sorts of questions about how our team planned to fund the acquisition, our timing for the initial public offering of FN, and aspects of our exit strategy. It must have worked because I snapped back to the reality of the situation and thought, "You must be joking. Here we are, snowshoeing up the side of a mountain, and he wants to talk about stock options, venture capital, and who knows what else!" But that was Chad.

He could see I was losing my mental stamina, and he also wanted some answers to several important questions. He loved to multitask so why not combine the two things he really loved: intense exercise and business. Chad is one of the most driven people I have ever met. His Q-and-A session also helped me maintain my focus and the relentless pursuit to Timberline Lodge. I kept urging myself forward by saying, "Come on. Keep pushing up the trail. If you stop, you will never get started again. You will pass out, and you will not be found until spring."

Then, Chad decided to try a tactic he thought would motivate me further; however, it was mostly demoralizing. He leaped ahead of me and began sprinting up the side of the mountain as if he were jogging in his snowshoes. I stopped and looked incredulously up at him. "What? How can you even do that?" I shouted up at him. I shook my head and kept trudging up the mountain.

Chad stopped and dug his poles and shoes deep into the snow and waited for me to catch up. After a couple of minutes, I finally reached his position. Chad smiled and said to me, "Whoa, buddy. We just burned a ton of calories making it up here, but we got a ways to go. You gonna make it?" I laughed and nodded. I was breathing too heavily for any more deep conversations. I dug my poles into the snow and sunk the spikes of my shoes into the trail. I reached down and pulled off the sweatshirt I had been wearing, and it was soaked with sweat. I tied it around my waist and turned to look back down the trail we had just climbed. Off in the distance I saw Mt. Jefferson, and it looked larger than life. It looked so close. I thought that if I got a running start, I could leap off Mt. Hood and land on the side of it. Little did I know that altitude plays games with distance perception because Mt. Jefferson is approximately 50 miles away from Mt. Hood.

Standing on the side of Mt. Hood gave me the opportunity to take in some of the most beautiful views I had ever seen firsthand. I was captivated by the impressive magnitude of this mountain and its awesome power.

And then we began our ascent again. It would have been easy to quit. It would have been easy to give up the relentless pursuit, but Chad would not let me quit. He would not let me give up. Chad knew that if he could motivate me to finish the climb, I would remember this day for the rest of my life. Chad pushed me to persevere, dig deeper than I ever had dug before in my life, and ignore the tremendous pain in my legs, back, and arms. He pushed me to focus on reaching the end of the trail. There were many times up that mountain that I heard Chad — typically from way out in front of me, too — yell back to me, "Come on Stephen, pick up the pace. Keep those arms and legs moving. Keep climbing. Keep climbing. Keep climbing, buddy!"

As we cleared the tree line, I thought, "Amen, we must be getting close." It was a miraculous sight when I finally saw Timberline Lodge. I had willed myself to achieve something I never would have considered possible. I had nothing left. I was mentally and physically exhausted. In that state of depletion, a quote from Coach Vince Lombardi made perfect sense to me. Coach Lombardi once said, "I firmly believe that any man's finest hour, the greatest fulfillment of all that he holds dear, is that moment when he has worked his heart out in a good cause and lies exhausted on the field of battle — victorious."

It is because of that morning on Mt. Hood, as well as other experiences in my life, that I firmly believe people's focus and their relentless pursuit of what they love and want most in this world are the keys to total happiness. Everything worth doing requires commitment, strategy, and hard work. A person needs to have a singular focus. Imagine you are pursing the one thing you have always wanted most in your life. There is no magic or secret that can grant us what we want most in this world. There are no shortcuts, and there are no second chances. We have to enjoy every opportunity we have.

The same goes for the viral social networking process I am about to share with you in this book. Yes, the process is efficient and effective, and yes, it will produce maximum results in the least amount of time, but it requires your focus and relentless pursuit of the business goals you are trying to accomplish. I assure you, there will absolutely be times when you want to quit or when you begin to question whether your time investment is going to pay off.

Trust me when I tell you that your time commitment will pay off. But, consistently communicating with the people in your social network takes time. It takes discipline to keep up with the conversation instead of leaving a flurry of posts and comments one week and then nothing for three to four weeks. This type of inconsistent communication will produce lackluster results.

You must relentlessly pursue your goals, never give up, keep fighting, and enjoy the total happiness that comes your way!

It is time to learn something new. It is time to challenge the status quo. Are you ready?

I wish you the best of success,

Stephen Woessner

INTRODUCTION

In my first book *The Small Business Owner's Handbook to Search Engine Optimization*, I shared my results-oriented, 15-step search engine optimization (SEO) process that provided all the tools necessary to increase a website's Google® search engine ranking in 30 days or fewer, as well as double site traffic in 90 days or fewer. The SEO process is centered on efficiency and effectiveness so you only need to invest time and energy toward steps that will deliver a measurable return on your investment. I approached the development of my 15-step viral social networking process with the same mindset — to make it as efficient and effective as possible. I want you to be able to implement the process and then move on to the other priorities on your to-do list for the day. You will get maximum results in the least amount of time if you follow this process.

I am confident that viral social networking will increase your online sales and website traffic because I have invested hundreds of hours toward practical research. I tested numerous theories, collected and analyzed data, and developed strategies for further testing until I perfected a social networking model that delivered impressive results. I set out on this quest because I wanted to know whether social networking could be used to quantifiably increase traffic to a website — and even more specifically, a small business website — while also increasing sales flowing through the website. My intuition told me that this seemed like a reasonable assumption, but I needed quantifiable evidence small business owners and managers could easily apply in very little time to become successful.

The next step was to invest seemingly endless hours of research, exploring what companies with successful and proven brands had achieved using social networking as a promotional tool. I scoured the best in peer-reviewed academic journals, newspapers, magazines, and any source I could get my hands on. I searched for proven strategies, models, and data points that would be useful in testing my social networking theory. I read and studied constantly. The following are some of the highlights I collected from my research:

> ▸ In a June 2009 story appearing in *Computerworld Magazine*, Dell Inc. said it uses social networking site Twitter™ to generate online sales. The company announced clearance sales and discount pricing with Twitter. Dell attributed $3 million of its total online sales of $61 billion to its Twitter use.

> ▸ Zappos.com uses Twitter to let its customers get to know its employees. A March 2009 story in *Computerworld Magazine* reported that of Zappos.com's 1,400 employees, about 450 use Twitter to promote the company. At the time of the article, Zappos.com CEO Tony Hsieh was the 20th most popular person on Twitter with more than 186,000 followers. As of November 2010, Hsieh had 1.7 million followers.

> ▸ The May 18, 2009 issue of *Advertising Age Magazine* reported that Naked Pizza, a New Orleans-based healthy pizza shop, used Twitter. The company began to track Twitter-related sales. In a test campaign run on April 23, it had a promotion announced exclusively via Twitter. The shop tracked every customer phone call and measured the source of every order. The Twitter-based promotion resulted in 15 percent of the day's business.

> ▸ A March 9, 2009 story appearing in *Brandweek Magazine* documented Papa John's experience using Facebook™. *Brandweek* reported how Papa John's gave anyone who became a "fan" of its Facebook profile an online code worth a free pizza. Within 24-hours, 131,000 people became fans of Papa John's. According to the *Brandweek* story, Papa John's was the second-fastest growing brand on Facebook in 2009.

As encouraging as this information was, the results all revolved around large companies with existing name recognition. Also, companies like Dell and Zappos.com were already generating significant revenue via online sales. In addition, the academic studies I researched used large companies as the model, were complex, and used complicated research methodologies and multivariate statistical analysis — all of which are not very useful for businesspeople who need to generate results in the least amount of time possible.

So, I began to question everything all over again. I wanted to know whether social networking success was reserved exclusively for large, well-known companies or if small- to mid-sized companies could also harness the apparent power of social networking as an online promotional tool. Although my research provided some good pieces of information that validated portions of my overall theory and gave me encouragement that I was headed in the right direction, none of the existing research either fully validated or contradicted my theory. To my surprise, no one had ever conducted a comprehensive study that specifically tested social networking's ability to affect change in both: 1) website traffic and 2) online sales. This left an exciting opportunity to extend the existing industry research by conducting a new study.

Now that I had my research foundation in place and knew what I wanted to test and evaluate, I decided to invest my time toward creating a social networking process that increased both online sales and website traffic. I felt confident my research would provide the necessary data to prove viral social networking's ability to increase website traffic and online sales. To begin the process, I launched a small business website (**www.seotrainingproducts. com**) with the help of Bernadot Studios (**www.bernadot.com**). The website was designed to help promote the publication of my first book and generate online sales of the book's companion DVD learning series.

Following the launch of my website, I began experimenting with many social networking steps and techniques on Facebook, Twitter, and LinkedIn˙. I made many mistakes and also experienced some successes throughout the duration of my research study. Ultimately, I collected and analyzed seven months of data from my website.

After analyzing the data, I concluded that viral social networking represented more than 23 percent of the traffic flowing into the website. Also, the conversion rate of online sales from traffic referred from the social networking sites Facebook, Twitter, and LinkedIn was 22 percent, versus the typical 2 to 4 percent from traditional traffic sources like organic, pay-per-click campaigns, or direct visits. This translates into a 780 percent increase of the online conversion rate. Viral social networking worked, and perhaps more importantly, it worked for a small business website.

My conclusion from the research, and my experience since the study concluded, has been that viral social networking can be used to deliver significant business benefits when someone follows a specific process using the right steps. These experiences formed the foundation of the 15 steps you will learn in this book. That makes this book a comprehensive guide to effective social networking for anyone looking for a practical strategy to increase online sales using Facebook, Twitter, and LinkedIn. The 15-step viral social networking process within this book is the same process I used to generate the results I described earlier. Nothing is held back. This book contains the full blueprint and all of the checklists you need to follow in order to be successful.

The 15 easy-to-follow steps in this book will also provide you with the tools you need to reduce your social networking time investment, while showing you how to measure results. I found methods and tools you can use to eliminate the number of hours involved so you can focus on managing your business as efficiently and effectively as possible.

We will get started by explaining the fundamentals of Facebook, Twitter, and LinkedIn. There are many more social networks, but these three represent the fastest growing sites with the most relevant audiences. The 15-step process is specifically devoted to these three networks. But, feel free to apply the 15-step process to other social networks if one fits your business niche specifically.

In addition, I will also share some criteria you can use when deciding which social networking site(s) are the best for your business goals. For example, is the potential audience on Twitter the right audience for your business? Would Facebook or LinkedIn be more appropriate? *See Chapter 1 for help with this process.*

What You Will Find in this Book

Chapter 1 will introduce you to what I call the "three Cs" of viral social networking: 1) creating conversation, 2) building community, and 3) generating commerce. Your proactive engagement and participation within viral social networking will bring you into the conversation. I suggest you get started by posting comments about your friends' or colleagues' posts or "status updates," after which they will begin doing the same to your posts. Soon enough, you will see that you have created an initial conversation(s).

All of the conversations you create help build your community. In addition, research studies have shown that active and robust social networks like the one you will build can morph into online brand communities. An online brand community is composed of people who possess a social identification with others who share their interests in a particular brand. Your online brand community could revolve around your business, your products and services, or a personal profile that becomes the brand. The personal-profile-brand strategy is similar to the way other successful entrepreneurs have become the "face" of their companies or organizations. Chapter 10 of this book includes a variety of success stories that will help you decide which strategy is ideal for you and your business goals.

Once your online brand community forms, you can then generate commerce through your posts, status updates, and the website content you share online. But, if you are like most businesspeople, you may wonder what things in your life or business are "that interesting" that they should be shared with the world via Facebook, Twitter, and LinkedIn. Sound familiar? Chapter 6 will help by providing you with suggested topic categories and recommendations about the type of content your social networking community will find interesting and valuable.

Developing the right content is only one piece in a viral social networking strategy. I included Chapter 7 to effectively demonstrate how to share your content with the social networking community you have worked so hard to build. You will also learn how to apply the proven 6:1 ratio of making six personal or life-related posts or status updates to your social networks for every one product- or service-related post. The 6:1 ratio will help you avoid the mistake of turning your viral social networks into a selling free-for-all.

And, how will you know if you have accomplished your goals? Chapter 9 will also demonstrate how to track and measure your performance using Google Analytics™ Web analytics service so you can observe how your efforts affect your site traffic and online sales.

In Chapter 10, I wrap up the book with the goal of helping you put the entire process together. I know that business owners have enough to deal with every single day so the thought of keeping their "viral social networking strategy" organized is the last priority on the list. Chapter 10 will help keep you focused because it summarizes all the steps into a tactical, action-oriented social networking checklist. This viral social networking blueprint will serve as your roadmap and can guide your daily to-do list. The chapter also includes frequently asked questions so you can benefit from the experiences of others.

I will never recommend steps or processes to you that I have not thoroughly tested and measured myself. I will also share the exact data I collected during all of my testing so you can see first-hand the power of the 15 steps in this viral social networking process. Nothing is hidden. I want you to have all of the knowledge you need to be immensely successful.

CHAPTER 1:

Your Social Networking Business Briefing

Viral social networking steps covered in this chapter:

▶ **Step 1:** Decide which social networks are ideal for your business goals.

There are many social networking-related terms you could invest plenty of time researching and studying, but nearly all of your time would be wasted. This book is not a conceptual exercise. Instead, I designed the 15 steps with the sole purpose of preparing you to hit the ground running. My goal is to help you become as efficient and effective as possible in the least amount of time. And besides, I have already spent countless hours researching social networking in its various forms, which has given me the ability to distill the unwieldy, confusing, and ridiculously technical jargon into a short list of the terms that will provide you with a solid foundation to maximize your results. Every businessperson looking to use social networking as a promotional tool for his or her business should understand the following:

1. **Social marketing:** Social marketing can be defined as the usage of marketing's four Ps — product, price, place, and promotion

— to achieve objectives that are related to some form of social good. For example, the current Pepsi™ Refresh project is an excellent example of social marketing. The company is funding a wide variety of grants across the country with the purpose of affecting positive change in the communities Pepsi serves. Social marketing is not the same as social networking, which is an important distinction from how the terms sometimes used to refer to the topics and the 15 steps within this book.

2. **Social networking:** Social networking services like Facebook, Twitter, and LinkedIn are all social networks. Clearly, there are many more social networks than these three. In fact, informal estimates say the number of social networks has reached 900 or more. This book will focus on these top three performers so you can maximum results in the least amount of time. The rationale for only selecting three networks will be discussed later in this chapter.

The purpose of social networks like Facebook, Twitter, and LinkedIn is to essentially facilitate building relationships among its members. Social networks make this happen by providing members with functional tools so they can share ideas, content, activities, events, opinions, and interests with the people in their individual networks.

Additionally, you might be interested to know there is something called social networking theory. This theory is used to identify the demographic similarities within social networks. For example, as the number of "friends" in your Facebook network increases, you will likely begin to notice demographic similarities — interests, occupations, ages, etc. Social networking theory is important to understand because the demographic similarity of your Facebook friends, Twitter followers, and LinkedIn connections will actually facilitate the transfer of the information and/or content you share. You might notice patterns regarding the type of people who respond to personal posts and the people who respond to posts of a professional nature. Understanding social networking theory and how people communicate in groups is important as you build your social network in Steps 5 and 6, and learn the steps for sharing your content with your networks. *See Chapter 7 for more information.*

The confusing aspect of the term social networking is that it is sometimes referred to as social media marketing, or the act of marketing or promoting oneself within the confines of a social network. Technically, the two terms can be used interchangeably.

3. **Social media:** Social media refers to the content created with the purpose of being disseminated through social networks like Facebook, Twitter, LinkedIn, and other sources. Social media comes in many different forms from simple website content pages, blog posts, photos, YouTube® video community videos, or podcasts. Steps 7 through 11 in this book involve several forms of social media and demonstrate how to distribute the content via your social networks.

4. **Viral marketing:** This promotional tactic involves the use of consumer-to-consumer — or peer-to-peer — communications, such as social networks to share information about a product or service in a manner that lends credibility to the product or service. The most common form of viral marketing occurs when consumers willingly become promoters of a product or service and spread the word to their friends. These people can be motivated to do so for financial rewards or simply out of their desire to share the product benefits with friends and

family. When done properly, viral marketing can facilitate the rapid adoption of new products in the marketplace because consumers tell all of their friends and family about their experience with a particular product. This is the essence of word-of-mouth advertising, and the value of it cannot be overstated.

Hotmail.com® is an incredible example of viral marketing success. Hotmail launched in 1996, and its initial users automatically promoted the service to everyone they e-mailed, simply by sending a message. This happened because each outgoing message included a link at the bottom of the message so the recipient could open his or her own free Hotmail account. The results were that 12 million Hotmail accounts were opened in just two years.

How Social Networking and Viral Marketing Create Viral Social Networking

I have termed the 15 steps viral social networking because the entire process revolves around the technology of social networks as defined before, and the steps are blended with aspects of viral marketing such as word-of-mouth (WOM) communications. This blending creates a powerful and influential promotional tool that increases online sales and website traffic. The following section aims to provide several highlights from the comprehensive research that was conducted to validate or contradict the hypothesis that viral social networking could be used as an effective promotional tool. I only shared highlights in this section because, although I get excited about the data, I realize that not everyone will share the same enthusiasm. Feel free to look me up on Facebook, Twitter, or LinkedIn if you want the full details.

I scoured dozens of top-quality academic research journals. These journals publish the work of the best and brightest academic minds all over the world. I found several sources that demonstrated how a company's activity within social networking sites, including viral marketing aspects like word-of-mouth communications, could help a company build an online brand community when a product for sale is the centerpiece of the company's social networking activity. I also dug into the research studies to see if I could determine whether a brand community could facilitate a consumer's decision-making process — product adoption — which is clearly the end goal.

Incidentally, this intensive research also helped me uncover a number of linkages that later formed the foundation for the three Cs in viral social networking: conversation, community, and commerce. The three Cs will be discussed in greater detail later in this chapter.

As discussed earlier, members of social networking sites use the technology to share information, collaborate, and interact with one another. Social networking sites also serve as arenas for consumers to share their reviews and preferences about products or services. When consumers share these reviews, the exchange of information becomes WOM communications because a product or service is the centerpiece of the message. WOM is a form of viral marketing.

A 2008 study conducted by De Bruyn and Lilien in the *International Journal of Research in Marketing* determined the effectiveness of WOM's role in the flow of information, as well as the flow of influence. From a marketing perspective, that makes WOM communications a very attractive part of the marketing mix because as an unpaid endorsement for products or services, WOM can be the most believable form of advertising. In addition, traditional media advertising seemingly continues to decline in effectiveness.

Advertising can be viewed as invasive clutter into the busy lives of consumers. Plus, which media should you select from the myriad of choices?

Want proof of the decline in the effectiveness of traditional media? Just look at Amazon.com™'s marketing mix. When was the last time you watched a TV commercial, heard a radio ad, or read a newspaper ad for Amazon.com? Amazon.com spends so little on traditional media because the company trusts the opinions of its consumers more than they do advertising, which makes the viral aspects of WOM communications so valuable.

But, do social networking activities like WOM necessarily result in the formation of a brand community? This can get a little complicated so this book will review each piece step-by-step. A 2004 study conducted by Dholakia, Bagozzi, and Pearo in the *International Journal of Research in Marketing* recognized online communities as consumer groups, many of which involve the discussions of specific products or product types. The researchers conducting the study identified these online groups as brand communities. Extending this point further, a 2008 study conducted by Thompson and Sinha in the *Journal of Marketing* concluded that brand communities could be viewed as social systems composed of members and communication channels through which information about new products is transmitted.

As mentioned earlier, brand communities are composed of people who possess a social identification with others who share their interest in a particular brand. In addition, brand communities are non-geographic, meaning they can exist anywhere — including on the Internet. This gives you the ability to use viral social networking to create a powerful and influential online brand community for your business.

Based on all of the data collected, it seemed reasonable to conclude that if brand communities are composed of people sharing common interests just like social networks, viral marketing activities like WOM communications are prominent within social networks, and brand communities can exist entirely online. Also, social networking sites have the potential to serve as the platform to develop an online brand community. Of course, the social networking activities must involve making a product or service the centerpiece.

De Bruyn and Lilien also suggested within their study that marketers could leverage the power of interpersonal relationships found between members of Facebook, Twitter, and LinkedIn to promote a product or service. The concept assumes that the electronic peer-to-peer communications, such as WOM, are an effective means to transform communication networks like social networks into influence networks. The networks could be used to capture recipients' attention and trigger interest, which could eventually lead to adoption or sales.

But, the effort needed to build an online brand community via social networking activities would only be valuable if the community positively affects the product adoption process. Therefore, it was necessary to quantifiably measure the effectiveness of a brand community's ability to increase online sales. Or, does an online brand community simply bring people together who have a common interest in a particular product or service?

I concluded that participation in a brand community built loyalty among members. For example, when a comparable product became available, longer-term membership in the brand community increased the likelihood of adopting products from the preferred brand and reduced the likelihood of adopting products from competing brands.

Based on these findings, participation within a brand community is likely to facilitate product adoption. Despite establishing what seems to be a reasonable relationship between brand communities, membership participation, and product adoption, I concluded that the existing research was somewhat limited with respect to measuring the direct effect of social networking activity on website traffic and online sales.

This is what motivated me to test my viral social networking theory by launching the website (**http://seotrainingproducts.com**) and collecting my own data.

Overviews, Popularity, and Member Demographics of Facebook, Twitter, and LinkedIn

The social networks I included within my research study were Facebook, Twitter, and LinkedIn. Each of these networks proved to be an effective promotional tool for increasing the number of "unique visitors" to SEOTrainingProducts. com. Unique visitors represent all of the individual people or visitors who visit your website during a given month, no matter how many times they visited your site during the same month. Each unique visitor only counts once and that is what you want. The goal is to identify how many individual people visit your website each month instead of ambiguous statistics like "hits," which are only an indication of how many times the individual graphics were accessed from your website. For example, if one of your website content pages contains five graphics — a company logo, three photos, and a banner ad promoting a special offer — each time a person loads that page in his or her browser, your traffic report will register five hits. So, it is possible for a very small number of people to generate a significant number of hits by simply browsing a website. This makes "hits" a completely irrelevant statistic. Unique visitors are the traffic measurement that matters most.

The traffic statistics provided by the company hosting your website likely already include the number of unique visitors your site receives on a monthly basis. If not, you should begin using Google Analytics™ (**www.google.com/analytics**) immediately. Google Analytics is free and provides an incredible amount of very relevant information. *See Chapter 9 for more information on Google Analytics.*

Now back to the overviews of Facebook, Twitter, and LinkedIn. Each network has its own unique demographics or member audience. You need to consider these differences when you develop and distribute content to the members of your online brand community. However, do not worry about content development and distribution at this point. Both will be covered in-depth during Step 7 through 12 of the 15-step process. For now, it is important to develop an understanding of Facebook, Twitter, and LinkedIn and the demographics of the members you will likely find using the networks.

The following section of this chapter pulls together an array of independent research sources to help give you a clear view of the three social networks. In addition, it provides you with a comprehensive understanding of the popularity of social networking in general. Although referenced several times within the next few pages, it is also recommend that you download your own copy of the *U.S. Digital Year in Review.* This informative and expertly written report was prepared by comScore. The company, which consists of a collection of analysts focused on predicting trends regarding online marketing, audience measurement, and various other digital marketing expertise, recently reported that social networking remained one of the

Web's top activities in 2009. You can download the free report at comScore's site (**www.comscore.com/digital09**).

ComScore reported that nearly four out of five Internet users visited a social networking site in December 2009. Social networking activity now represents at least 11 percent of all time spent online in the United States. This makes social networking one of the most engaging activities across the Internet. In addition, this massive popularity of social networks applies to more than just generations X and Y. The following section details how the largest and fastest growing age segments are adults older than 35.

According to comScore, 2009 was a landmark year in the United States social networking market, as Facebook surged to the No. 1 position for the first time in May and continued its strong growth trajectory throughout the year. Facebook finished 2009 with 112 million visitors during the month of December 2009. This represented a 105 percent increase during the year.

Twitter finished the year with nearly 20 million members. This was a large increase from just 2 million visitors the previous year. Much of Twitter's extraordinary audience growth occurred during the first few months of 2009, and at one point, membership jumped from 4 million members to 17 million members between February and April 2009.

As a marketer, I cannot think of another media opportunity available to businesses that can duplicate or even come close to delivering the same audience growth or engagement level as what social networking can provide. Now we will take a closer look at the three networks individually.

Facebook overview

I included Facebook as part of my strategy because it became the No. 1 social network in 2009 as reported by comScore. In addition to comScore, other respected media have studied and reported on Facebook's rapid growth and usage rates. For example, the July 23, 2009 issue of *The Economist* reported that Facebook had increased its membership from 100 million in August 2008 to approximately 300 million at the time of the article. As I write this chapter, Facebook has even more members. The most recent estimate was more than 500 million. In addition, a January 2009 Compete.com study ranked Facebook as the most used social network by worldwide monthly active users.

In addition to Facebook's surging population of users, comScore reported that the social networking site grew across nearly every performance metric during 2009. Unique visitors, page views, and total time spent on Facebook all increased by a factor of two or more. Frequency metrics, such as average minutes used per day — up 6 percent — and average usage days per visitors — up 37 percent — also increased. As more people use Facebook more frequently, the site has grown to account for three times as much total time spent online as it did last year.

Facebook was founded in 2004 by Mark Zuckerberg along with his college roommates and fellow computer science students Eduardo Saverin, Dustin Moskovitz, and Chris Hughes. Facebook's membership was initially limited by the founders to Harvard students but was expanded to other colleges in the Boston area, the Ivy League, and Stanford University. Facebook later expanded further to include any university student, then high school students, and finally, to anyone older than 13.

Facebook members can create profiles with their personal photos, lists of interests, contact information, as well as any other personal information they feel like sharing. Facebook is an outstanding facilitator of communication. Facebook enables members to communicate with friends and other users through private or public messages or via its "chat" feature. Facebook members can also create and join interest groups including "Like™ pages," which were formerly called "fan pages" until April 19, 2010. "Like" or "fan" pages are maintained by organizations or businesses as a promotional tool. Online privacy continues to be a top concern; therefore, Facebook enables its members to choose their own privacy settings and select who can view the various parts of their profile.

One of the typical misconceptions about social networking activity is that it is reserved for generations Y or younger, especially because Facebook grew from its beginnings on college campuses and later spread to high school students. But, the largest percent of membership, and the fastest growing segment, has been adults older than 35.

In fact, Facebook's target audience is definitely adults, not youths. According to iStrategyLabs, Facebook watched its United States-based members grow from 42 million in 2008 to 103 million in 2009, which is a 144.9 percent increase. More importantly for Facebook's usage as a business promotional tool, Facebook members who are within the adults 35 years and older segment now represent more than 30 percent of the entire Facebook member base. In addition, the 55 years and older segment grew by an impressive 922.7 percent in 2009. Facebook's audience was distributed almost evenly between members older and younger than 35 years old. The most noticeable shift within Facebook's membership occurred with 25 to 34 year olds. According to comScore, this age segment represented 23 percent of Facebook's total membership in December 2009. This is an increase of 4.2 percent over the 18.8 percent total in 2008.

The numbers delivered by Facebook are astonishing. The social networking site is experiencing record growth, and from a marketer's perspective, Facebook seems to represent the ideal audience for a business to target. Facebook's audience and growth rate justify its consideration as a promotional tool.

Twitter overview

Also included is Twitter — the popular micro-blogging site at **www.twitter. com** — as part of the social networking strategy because according to Twitter's official website, there are currently 125 million registered users, which obviously pales in comparison to Facebook's 500 million. One of the main criticisms against Twitter is that many of the people with accounts are not Tweeting. For example, a study by RJMetrics published in *Computerworld Magazine* showed that only 17 percent of account holders Tweeted during the month of December 2009. This speaks to the importance of remaining consistent with your viral marketing strategy. *See Chapter 7 for more information.* Overall, Twitter was ranked as the third most used social network in February 2009 by Compete.com.

Statistics that measure the usage duration of Twitter members is not currently available. But, there is the somewhat accepted characteristic that Twitter's members tend to be more mobile than the members of other social networking site, or at least mobile while using Twitter. For some reason, Twitter members tend to prefer using the social networking site while they are mobile. This level of active and mobile engagement tends to make responses a Tweet™ seem, at times, nearly instantaneous.

According to the comScore report cited earlier, Twitter's overall audience grew in 2009. In addition, the social networking site experienced some shifts in its demographic composition. All demographic segments achieved substantial gains in visitors, but certain segments grew more rapidly than others. The initial success of Twitter was largely driven by users in the 25 to 54 age segment, which made up 65 percent of all visitors to the site in December 2008, with 18 to 24 year olds accounting for just 9 percent of visitors.

This older-age skew varied dramatically from the traditional social media early adopter model, in which younger users tend to drive the majority of usage. Despite Twitter's initially older skew, as it gained widespread popularity with the help of celebrity Tweeters and mainstream media coverage, younger users flooded to the social networking site. According to comScore, Twitter members younger than 18 — up 6.2 percentage points in 2009 — and 18 to 24 year olds — up 7.9 percentage points — represent the fastest growing demographic segments.

Quantcast® is a company that provides detailed audience profiles for the advertising marketplace to learn more about what consumers are doing online. Quantcast focuses on measuring and organizing the world's audiences in real-time so advertisers can buy, sell, and connect with those audiences who are the most relevant. In April 2010, Quantcast published a demographic report regarding Twitter's members. Twitter's popularity among people 18 years or older is substantial with 82 percent of its total members belonging to that segment. In addition, 38 percent of Twitter's members are in the over 35 segment. Here are some highlights:

Gender:

- Males: 45 percent

▸ Females: 55 percent

Age Segments:

▸ 13 to 17 year olds represents 14 percent of membership

▸ 18 to 34 year olds represents 45 percent of membership

▸ 35 to 49 year olds represents 24 percent of membership

▸ Older than 50 represents 14 percent of membership

From an income perspective, Twitter members tend to earn an above average income, with 58 percent earning at least $60,000 per year. But, apparently income does not correlate to education for the site's users because 49 percent of Twitter members have not attended college.

You can find additional Twitter statistics from Quantcast's website (**www.quantcast.com/twitter.com/demographics#summary**).

The numbers delivered by Twitter are impressive; although, the network is substantially smaller than Facebook. However, the audience tends to be more mobile. This facilitates the rapid and/or viral dissemination of content within the social network making Twitter a very valuable tool for spreading timely information. Twitter's features justify its consideration as a promotional tool.

LinkedIn overview

I included LinkedIn as part of my social networking strategy because of the social networking site's superb business-oriented demographic. LinkedIn had approximately 90 million users spanning 200 countries as of October 2009. But, according to LinkedIn's statistics found on their advertising center, the site's membership has declined to 80 million as of November 2010.

The fact that LinkedIn's membership base is declining is cause for concern, but the demographics of LinkedIn's membership are quantifiably the most business-oriented when compared to Facebook and Twitter.

One of the distinct advantages that LinkedIn provides marketers is the data it offers regarding its usage among members who hold management-level positions and who have above average household income (HHI) levels. For example, 32.1 percent of LinkedIn members hold middle management or higher positions and a staggering 51.8 percent of members have total HHIs of $100,000 or more. The demographic data in Figure 1.1 shows that LinkedIn members are educated, possess above average HHI, and likely hold decision-making positions within their respective organizations.

Figure 1.1 LinkedIn member demographics

	LinkedIn Comp | Reach	WSJ Comp | Reach	Forbes Comp | Reach	BusinessWeek Comp | Reach
Male / Female	54% / 46%	64% / 36%	67% / 33%	58% / 42%
Average Age	43	50	50	48
Average HHI	$107,278	$99,911	$96,003	$95,255
▪ $100k+	51.8 | 6,467,006	43.2 | 3,599,000	39.5 | 3,442,000	38.8 | 1,440,000
▪ $150k+	23.1 | 2,888,000	22.7 | 1,692,000	20 | 1,741,000	19.2 | 712,000
Education				
▪ College/Post Grad	77.6 | 9,697,000	69.7 | 5,802,000	65.5 | 5,709,000	66.6 | 2,468,000
▪ Post College Graduate	39.8 | 4,967,000	37.7 | 3,135,000	33.6 | 2,926,000	36.2 | 1,341,000
Senior-Level Management				
▪ EVP/SVP/VP	6.2 | 770,000	5.3 | 438,000	3.7 | 324,000	5.1 | 189,000
▪ Senior Management	14.1 | 1,761,000	15.8 | 1,318,000	12.8 | 1,117,000	13.2 | 490,000
▪ Middle Management or above	32.1 | 4,012,000	26.6 | 2,216,000	23.6 | 2,058,000	26.7 | 991,000

LinkedIn also provides some excellent insight into its audience by segmenting its members into the following categories:

1. **Small and medium business professionals:** Members who are working in buisnesses with between 50 and 500 employees. LinkedIn estimates that more than 3.7 million of its members are in the small to medium-sized business category.

2. **Business decision-makers:** Members who hold the title of "director" or above at any size company. LinkedIn estimates that more than 7 million of its members are in the decision-maker category.

3. **Financial service professionals:** Members who work in the financial services industry. LinkedIn estimates that more than 7.5 million of its members are in the financial services category.

4. **Sales professionals:** Members who have identified their job function as being sales related. LinkedIn estimates that more than 2.8 million of its members are in the sales category.

5. **Marketing professionals:** Members who have identified themselves as working in the marketing and advertising industry. LinkedIn estimates that more than 3.5 million of its members are in the marketing and advertising category.

6. **Startup professionals:** Members who are currently working at companies who employ between one to 50 people. LinkedIn estimates that more than 3.2 million of its members are in this category.

7. **Corporate executives:** Members who have identified themselves as holding the position of "director" or higher at companies with more than 500 employees. LinkedIn estimates that more than 2 million of its members are in this category.

8. **IT professionals:** Members who have identified their job responsibilities as being IT or engineering related. LinkedIn estimates that more than 5.5 million of its members are in this category.

9. **Career changers:** Members who have recently changed their job responsibilities or employers within the last 60 days. LinkedIn estimates that more than 970,000 of its members are in this category.

LinkedIn is also the only social network among the three that was evaluated as part of the strategy in this book that offers both a free and paid version. The paid versions of LinkedIn cost $24.95, $49.95, or $499.95 per month, and the features of each are explained in detail on the LinkedIn website (**www. linkedin.com**). I did not use any of these plans. I only used LinkedIn's free version. Based on my experience, as well as all of the social networking-related conversations I have had with industry experts and other businesspeople, I have never heard anyone advocate the paid versions of LinkedIn. In my opinion, LinkedIn's free account provides ample features and benefits.

In my opinion, LinkedIn's demographics made using its network for the dissemination of business-oriented content an important piece of my viral social networking strategy. My conclusion based on this data was that LinkedIn's high-targeted audience justifies its inclusion as a promotional tool.

Now that you have a solid foundation of the member demographics and growth rates of Facebook, Twitter, and LinkedIn, it is time to review how viral social networking creates the three Cs.

The Three Cs of Viral Social Networking

There are three "Cs" that form as a result of viral social networking. They are: 1) creating conversation, 2) building community, and 3) generating commerce.

Getting involved and creating the conversation is the way viral social networking begins. An efficient and effective way to start your journey is to set up your free Facebook, Twitter, and LinkedIn accounts. *Chapters 2, 3, and 4 of this book have been designed to assist you in that process.*

Once your Facebook, Twitter, and LinkedIn accounts are properly setup, you should begin experimenting and learning how each of the social networks can help you interact with people you already know. You can do this by completing your profile(s), sending friend requests, chatting with people, and writing "wall" posts to get used to the technology. And yes, you will likely make some mistakes as you get started, but you will probably be pleasantly surprised at how easy it is to get involved with social networking and creating your own conversations.

As you invite more people into your social networks, and as you accept invitations from others, you will begin to build an online brand community that revolves around you, your business, and the conversations you have created. A brand community is simply a collection of people who share common interests, and as discussed earlier in this chapter, brand communities can exist 100 percent online. With each new friend request you send out or accept, your community will grow. Successful online communities are the ones that tap into three basic needs of human nature: 1) People want to belong, 2) people want to make a difference in the world, and 3) people want to be heard. Creating and facilitating conversations among the members of your online brand community satisfies all three of these basic needs.

As you contribute and create conversations among the members of your community, an incredible thing happens: Your participation begins to build engagement, or a close bond, between you and the members of your community. This engagement or bond is sometimes referred to as "tie strength." For example, as members of your community become more familiar with one another and interactions increase, the relationships between members increase in familiarity or strength (tie). If the tie strength between members A and B is high, member A might decide to share a recommendation regarding a product or service with member B. In addition, if there is tie strength between the two members, there is a higher likelihood that member B will purchase the recommended product because member A was the source. Member A is someone who member B trusts because of the tie strength. *Step 11 in Chapter 7 focuses specifically on building trust and genuine relationships with your online brand community members.*

Building a trust-oriented community can produce tie strength and set the foundation for generating commerce, the final C of viral social networking. As in the example of members A and B, you can begin to generate commerce by making some product or service recommendations regarding the products or services your company sells. Or, you could also recommend other products or services you are passionate about, such as recent movies you have seen, books you have read, or some of your favorite restaurants. Then, watch your conversations among community members develop and expand to include additional community members. Follow this by placing a link to your website within a status update you post, and then watch the number of unique visitors to your website increase. *In Chapter 9, you will learn how to determine whether the increase in unique visitors originated from your online brand community so you can directly measure your viral social networking results.*

In addition, you will likely notice an increase in online sales if you have a product or service you already sell online. Use this simple ratio: You should make six personal or life-related posts or status updates for every one product or service-related post. *See Chapter 7 for more information on the 6:1 ratio.*

By following the 6:1 ratio, you will keep your conversations genuine and avoid the temptation to turn your online brand community into a selling free-for-all, which would be a major mistake.

The first portion of this chapter defined social networking and viral networking and explained how they blend together to form viral social networking. The overviews of Facebook, Twitter, and LinkedIn were designed to provide you with a broad familiarization with each social network that would be helpful when developing your viral social networking strategy. And, the discussion of the three Cs is the perfect foundation that transitions you into the final section of this chapter, which is Step 1 of the process: deciding which social networks are ideal for your business goals.

Step 1: Decide which Social Networks are Ideal for Your Business Goals

The selection of the social networks that best align with your business goals is Step 1 because it is the strategic foundation of the entire viral social networking process. Making the right decisions now will help you avoid investing time toward markets that do not align with your business goals.

Do you remember what I shared earlier in the Preface as I wrapped up the Mt. Hood story? I said that success requires your focus and relentless pursuit. It is important to make sure you apply your focused attention and relentless pursuit toward the networks that represent the greatest opportunity of success for you and your business. Otherwise, you will miss the opportunity to maximize your efficiency and effectiveness.

A friend once told me, "Stephen, a person's business makes money by doing business with people who know them, by doing business with people who like them, and by doing business with people who trust them." Based on my experience from owning four businesses, as well as working with hundreds of clients, I would have to completely agree with this statement. Our mission should be to select the social networks that will efficiently and effectively achieve all three of these basic business objectives.

There are many more, but the following are eight typical business goals as they relate to online marketing:

1. Increase unique website visitors from X to Y

2. Increase online sales from X to Y

3. Increase the duration — amount of time — your visitors spend within your website

4. Increase the number of e-newsletter subscribers

5. Decrease the amount spent on traditional advertising

6. Decrease the amount spent on Google AdWords™ advertising services campaigns

7. Increase website traffic to an associated blog

8. Expand the customer base by reaching new demographics or geographic territories

Overall, my recommendation is to begin relentlessly pursing your business goals by starting small and focusing on mastering this 15-step process as it relates to one network at first. This is especially true if you are relatively new to social networking. Honestly, it will not take you long to master the use of one social network. Once you have mastered your first network, you can then easily blend more networks into your strategy.

I recommend that you start small because I have witnessed so many business owners and managers who are excited about the opportunities that viral social networking represent make the mistake of taking on too many projects at one time. As a result, these people became overwhelmed with the prospects of building and managing their profiles across multiple networks. Despite their good intentions, these people found it difficult to get much done because their minds were swimming with tasks. Resist the temptation of feeling like you need to master Facebook, Twitter, and LinkedIn simultaneously. Focusing on too many priorities before you are adequately prepared will only create stress for you, as well as greatly inhibit your opportunities for success.

So, which social networks best align with the eight business goals previously mentioned? First, I recommend that you make Facebook the center of your viral social networking strategy regardless of the type of business you own or manage. I also recommend beginning the process with Facebook regardless of your typical customer demographic. This recommendation is based on the Facebook overview, impressive popularity, and member data presented earlier in this chapter. Facebook offers business owners the opportunity to tap into the largest and fastest growing social networking audience on the planet that is also the most demographically varied.

Facebook also represents a tremendous opportunity to share personal information with your customers and prospects. If you are looking to develop an online brand community, then Facebook needs to be part of your strategy. It is the only one of the three social networks discussed in this book where you can share photos, videos, and other forms of content with your members to create deep personal relationships and trust. Whether your business sells directly to consumers or directly to businesses, Facebook would be an ideal selection.

The decision of whether to include Twitter and LinkedIn into your viral social networking strategy is a bit more complex.

Twitter is essentially a micro-blog that is all about real-time and consistent updates. The successful people using Twitter tend to send Tweets about five to six times a day. This can become time consuming, but Twitter is effective at increasing website traffic, and the traffic that flows from Twitter is nearly instantaneous because Twitter followers are more mobile and they carry Twitter with them. So, if your business is looking for an additional medium to announce special deals, promotions, or giving someone a moment-by-moment look into events, performances, and so on, then Twitter would be an ideal selection.

LinkedIn is the leading business-oriented professional network, which makes it ideal for anyone selling products or services directly to businesses. The opportunity to share and distribute content is limited but targeted because of the demographics of the network. I do not recommend investing time toward building an online brand community using LinkedIn if you own a business that is strictly focused on individual consumers. For example, if you own a retail store or other form of consumer-related service business, investing time toward building a LinkedIn profile would not be an efficient and effective use of your time.

LinkedIn's business-oriented demographic make the social network ideal for companies that provide professional services, such as accounting, finance, marketing, strategic consulting, and continuing education.

In summary, Facebook will likely serve as the cornerstone of your strategy. With respect to Twitter and LinkedIn, select the one that most closely aligns with your business goals — and perhaps both networks do.

The fundamentals of Facebook will be covered in depth within Chapter 2. You will want to study the Twitter fundamentals in Chapter 3 if you have decided to add Twitter to your strategy. Otherwise, feel free to skip that chapter. You will want to study the LinkedIn fundamentals in Chapter 4 if you have decided to add LinkedIn to your strategy. Otherwise, feel free to skip that chapter and proceed to Chapter 5.

Viral Social Networking Checklist: Part 1

❏ Become familiar with the three Cs.

❏ Create an initial list of viral social networking goals you would like to accomplish. For your reference, Step 1 includes a quick list of typical business goals that you might want to consider.

❏ Complete Step 1 by making your final selection of social networks for your strategy.

CHAPTER 2:

Facebook Fundamentals

Viral social networking steps covered in this chapter:

▸ **Step 2:** Get started with Facebook.

As viral social networkers, we will not be using Facebook as a social entertainment tool — although it certainly serves that purpose for millions of people. This book will not teach you how to play Facebook games like the popular Mafia Wars or Farmville. In addition, we will not invest time toward learning the myriad of interactive applications that exist.

Instead, our top priority will be to utilize Facebook's social networking platform to efficiently and effectively influence and persuade a portion of the 500 million Facebook members. Bottom line: Our goal with Facebook, as well as Twitter and LinkedIn, is to create genuine conversations, build an online brand community revolving around you and/or your products and services, and ultimately, generate commerce through online sales and website traffic.

This chapter is not intended to be a comprehensive Facebook manual. The goal of this chapter is to help you become familiar, comfortable, and proficient within the Facebook social network as quickly as possible so you can begin creating conversation, building community, and generating commerce.

Creating Your Facebook Account

Now, it is time for you to create your free account on Facebook.com, assuming you have not already done so. Begin by opening any Web browser — such as Internet Explorer®, Mozilla Firefox®, or Google Chrome™ Web browsers — and go to Facebook's website (**www.facebook.com**). Completing the account creation process is quick because you simply need to fill in the six pieces of information requested on Facebook's home page: 1) first name, 2) last name, 3) e-mail address, 4) password, 5) gender, and 6) birthday. Facebook requires a date of birth because it is the company's way of encouraging authenticity and providing only age-appropriate content. But, once you create your account, you can change your privacy settings to hide your birthday from other Facebook members if you like.

Click the green "Sign Up" button under the birthday fields once you have entered in the requested information. The screen that follows will confirm that you have completed Step 1 of the Facebook setup process, and it will prompt you to begin finding friends.

Finding Facebook Friends

Facebook's Find Friends feature has the capability to search your e-mail account — Microsoft Outlook®, Gmail™ Webmail service, and Yahoo! ® Mail, for example — and collect all of the e-mail addresses in your contacts list. Facebook will then compare those e-mail addresses with its current member list and recommend people you should consider sending "friend request" invitations. The Find Friends feature is very helpful, and it makes building your initial list of friends efficient.

You can use the Find Friends feature by entering your e-mail address and e-mail account password. Please note: Facebook states that they do not store e-mail account passwords, which protects the security of your e-mail account. Click the blue "Find Friends" button once you have entered your e-mail address and password. Facebook will then display a list of people you know who are already using Facebook.

Assuming that Facebook has properly matched your contacts' e-mail addresses, you will be able to "friend" people by simply clicking the "Add as Friend" link shown to the right of each person who was matched from your contact list. The recipient of your friend request will have to confirm your relationship before that person officially becomes your friend on Facebook.

The people to whom you send friend requests will receive a notification from Facebook. The notification message informs them that they have received a friend request and who sent the request. When the recipient opens the notification, he or she will see your name and profile photo. From the notification screen, the recipient can accept the friend request by clicking the blue "Confirm" button, or they can ignore the request by clicking the gray "Ignore" button. In addition, the recipient can also choose to send a message back to you.

Completing Your Facebook Profile

After completing the initial round of friend requests, Facebook will prompt you to complete your profile by requesting that you enter the names of your high school, college/university, and employer. When you enter this information, Facebook will make additional friend suggestions to you by matching your information with other Facebook members. In addition, this information will be added to your profile. All of the information can be edited or deleted from your profile in the future whenever you like.

Once Step 2 of the setup process is complete, Facebook will walk you through the process of providing five additional pieces of information that can be used to complete your profile. The additional information is optional. You can upload a profile picture, enter your profile information, activate your mobile phone so you can use Facebook Mobile if you choose to, find additional people you may know, and adjust your privacy settings.

The information section within your account that might require the most time for you to fill out is the profile section. To access this section, click on the gray "Edit Profile" button.

Editing your profile provides opportunities to share as much or as little about yourself as you like. My recommendation is to make your profile as detailed as possible so your Facebook friends can get a true sense of who you are. It is also important to be truthful and genuine, which will also help you develop closer relationships with your Facebook friends because they will know the real you. Never be fake or disingenuous.

Your profile information can be easily edited whenever you like in the future so do not worry that you will somehow be tied to the information you enter right now. Once you complete this section and click the blue "Save Changes" button at the bottom of the screen, Facebook will display your information in two different areas within your profile. Underneath your profile photo, Facebook will include links that read, "View Photos of Me" and "View Videos of Me." These links make it easy for your friends to see photos and videos where you appear. Creating photo albums and "tagging" yourself in photos and videos will be discussed later in this chapter.

Now look directly under your two links. Here, you have an opportunity to write a short, several-sentence bio about yourself. For example, my short bio reads "Author of *The Small Business Owner's Handbook to Search Engine Optimization.*" This is the title of the first book I wrote, and I want every person who has access to my profile to have easy access to the book title. Beneath the snippet of text, Facebook provides your friends with a glimpse of the profile information you just finished entering. It has been my experience that the more detailed the information is that you share about yourself, the greater success you will have in building strong relationships.

Updating Your Facebook Profile Photo

One of the most critical aspects of your Facebook profile is the photo you decide to use. Your photo acts as the visual connection between you and your target audience. I have seen many people on Facebook use photos of their children or pets as their profile photos. Although photos like this can be very personal, the photos are not of you, and presenting yourself to your target audience is critically important. But, you should absolutely share photo albums of family, friends, pets, scenic shots from vacations, and so on within the "photos" section of your profile. I will show you how to add and manage your photos later in this chapter.

For your profile photo, I recommend choosing a shot that is the closest representation of your everyday life. I recommend selecting a professional, yet still casual pose. I hired a professional photographer to shoot my Facebook profile photo because I wanted something professional but still casual.

I will now walk you through how to add your profile photo to replace the light blue and white silhouette placeholder image that Facebook uses to represent your profile photo until you replace it with an actual photo.

To upload an actual profile photo, simply click on the silhouette placeholder image, or the "Upload a Photo" link locate beneath the image.

From this screen, you will want to click on the "Change Profile Picture" link. This will take you to a screen where you can browse your hard drive for the photo you want to use as your profile photo. You can also choose to add multiple profile photos if you like. Facebook only allows you to display one photo at a time within your profile. But, your friends can still browse all of the profile photos you have uploaded because they will be available within a "Profile Pictures" album that Facebook creates for you automatically. Once you have finished uploading your profile photo(s), you will receive a screen that displays all of the photos available in your profile. Now, you simply select which photo you want to display on your profile page. You can change or update your profile photo as often as you like.

Facebook Account and Privacy Settings

Customizing your "Account" and "Privacy" settings is the final step before you begin learning how to write on your wall, post comments, create photo albums, chat with friends, and send inbox messages. You can access your account settings by clicking the "Account" link in the upper right corner of the Facebook screen. Clicking the "Account" link will reveal a drop down menu that includes six options: 1) Edit Friends, 2) Account Settings, 3) Privacy Settings, 4) Application Settings, 5) Help Center, and 6) Logout. Click on "Account Settings."

The account settings section allows you to adjust the name you used when creating your account, update your password, set your e-mail address, and change several security settings. From this screen, I recommend that you click on the "Manage" link to the right of the "Privacy" section. Once clicked, Facebook will take you to its privacy settings screen where you can manage your settings in several categories. The privacy settings are something you should give substantial consideration to because these settings determine who can access the information within your profile. For example, do you only want to allow friends to be able to see your personal information and posts? You have the option of allowing "Everyone," "Friends and Networks," "Friends of Friends," "Friends Only," and "Customize."

Even though my goal has been to build as robust of an online brand community as possible, I still set my privacy settings to "Only Friends." I did this so I could be somewhat assured that I have a reasonable level of relationship or familiarity with the people who I grant access to my family photos, profile information, and other personal details. However, this is a personal decision. You will have your own comfort level for what you feel is appropriate for you. It might be more or less conservative than what I decided to use. You need to weigh the options, trade-offs, and make the decision that feels comfortable to you. Regardless of what you decide, all of the information in your profile, as well as the security settings, can be updated and revised in the future no matter what you select during the account setup process.

Writing Your First Facebook Status Update

Facebook includes a wall feature, which is simply a repository of all of your status updates, comments your friends decide to write on your wall, links to the content you upload, and so forth. The account privacy settings you selected control the access of who can post content on your wall, which is also known as writing on someone's wall, or even view your wall. I have "Only Friends" selected as my privacy setting so only the people I have decided to accept or invite as friends can post comments on my wall.

One of the main aspects of your wall is what is called status updates. Facebook places your status update directly to the right of your profile photo. In very small text under your status update, Facebook will place the date you posted your status update.

To write a status update on your wall, simply type your thoughts into the empty field that reads, "What's on your mind?"

When you are happy with what you have written, click the blue "Share" button beneath the field. Once the "Share" button is clicked, the new status update will be shared with your friends via their "news feed."

The status updates you add to your wall are also featured within what Facebook calls the news feed feature. The news feed feature essentially acts as the great aggregator of content. It displays and organizes all of your friends' most recent status updates and other content postings on their walls into one continuously updated live stream of content. You can see and read what is going on in the lives of your friends with a simply click of the mouse. You can access your news feed by clicking the "Home" link in the upper right corner of the Facebook screen.

Learning how to write and post a status update on your wall is sufficient for right now. Later, this book will demonstrate how you can incorporate some really interesting content into your status updates, including direct links to website content pages and video files to share great content with your online brand community. *See Chapter 6 for more information.* I will also demonstrate how to write effective and persuasive status updates that will encourage your friends to post comments or post their reaction to what your status update included.

Writing on a Friend's Facebook Wall

One of the best ways to stay in touch with your Facebook friends is to write/ post a comment on their walls. But, this assumes they have set their privacy settings to allow friends to post comments. I have several friends who have decided to block access to anyone posting comments on their walls. It has been my experience, and will likely be yours, too, that most people allow their friends to write comments on their walls.

When you write on a friend's wall, he or she can choose to respond by writing a comment to your wall post. To do so, he or she would simply click on the blue "Comment" link directly under your wall post, write his or her response, and click the blue "Comment" button that Facebook makes available. His or her comment would be posted directly underneath your original wall post.

The benefit to wall posts and the subsequent comments is how they create conversations. Posts create conversation because if you comment on someone's status update, every person who also comments on the status update will receive an e-mail or other form of notification with the contents of your comment. In addition, when other people comment after you comment, you will receive all subsequent comments via e-mail or other form of notification.

This is important to do to keep the conversation flowing. Some people will ask you questions within your comments, and it is important to answer the questions or the conversation dwindles. In addition, as more people write comments, momentum builds and more people jump into the conversation.

In addition to writing comments regarding someone's wall post, or the subsequent comments from others, you can also chose to "like" a post. This is the easiest way to contribute to a conversation without having to write anything creative. All you need to do is simply click the "Like" button to the immediate right of the "Comment" link. Once you click the link, a message will appear next to the comment you liked that reads, "You Like this." The fact that you liked a post or other form of content will also appear in your the news feed, as well as the feeds of all your Facebook friends.

Are you beginning to see the viral aspects of social networking within the Facebook community? Each conversation created has the potential of spurring many subconversations on the same topic or even completely different topics. More importantly, the conversations you create help build the online brand community discussed in Chapter 1 of this book. Creating conversations, and participating in the existing conversations of your friends, is critical to your success.

Inbox Messages

Facebook also comes with its own internal communication system called the inbox. You can send messages to anyone on Facebook, but most people use it to remain in contact with their Facebook friends. Inbox messages are private and only received by the friends you select as the recipients. Inbox messages will never appear on someone's wall or as a comment to a post.

To write an inbox message, simply click on the "Messages" link in the upper left navigation of the Facebook window. There are three blue icons, and the messages icon is the one in the middle. Facebook's navigation design makes seeing some of the icons a bit of a challenge. Once clicked, Facebook will provide you with a new message window.

Begin typing in your friend(s) name(s) in the "To:" field, and Facebook will self-populate a list of names for you to select from based on the first several letters you typed into the field. Then, write the remainder of your message just like you would an e-mail. You can also attached links, video files, or other content to the inbox messages you send. When you finish writing your message, click the blue "Send" button, and the message will be sent to the recipients you selected. Typically, the recipients receive a notification within their Facebook account, as well as a standard e-mail with the contents of the inbox message. The recipient can then log in to their Facebook account and reply.

Creating A Facebook Official Page for Your Business

You might have considered creating a Facebook account for your business. Facebook used to call business pages "Fan" pages. These were renamed as "official" pages. Developing an Official Facebook Page for your business could be a good strategy, but I recommend that you focus your attention right now developing your personal profile. I believe you are more apt to be successful in developing tie strength with your community as a person versus a business. In my opinion, official pages are impersonal and are almost counterproductive to the purpose of viral social networking. Because of this, I have not covered the creation of official pages in this chapter. But, there is certainly nothing wrong with having both types of Facebook pages. You can create your Official Facebook Page by visiting **www.facebook.com/pages/create.php**.

Viral Social Networking Checklist: Part 2

❏ Sign up for your free Facebook account.

❏ Send out friend requests using Facebook's "Find Friends" feature.

❏ Fill out your profile information, and make it as detailed as possible — and be genuine.

❏ Upload a professional but casual photo, and select it for your profile.

❏ Adjust your account and privacy settings to match your comfort level for security.

❏ Become familiar with writing on your own Wall by completing your first status update.

❏ Become familiar with writing on a friend's Wall by writing your first comment on someone else's Wall.

❏ Become familiar with writing comments by contributing to the conversation taking place on someone else's Wall.

❏ Become familiar with "liking" content by clicking the "Like" link underneath someone else's Wall post or comment.

❏ Become familiar with writing inbox messages by sending a message to one of your friends.

❏ Proceed to Chapter 3: Twitter Fundamentals.

Twitter Fundamentals

Viral social networking steps covered in this chapter:

▸ **Step 3**: Get started with Twitter.

Welcome to Twitter fundamentals. Chapter 3 will provide you with all of the information necessary to enable you to effectively use Twitter to create genuine conversation, build your online brand community and business network, and ultimately, generate commerce through online sales. As was the case with the focus of Chapter 2 concerning Facebook fundamentals, this chapter is not intended to be a comprehensive Twitter manual. If you would like additional details regarding the inter-workings of Twitter, I highly recommend reading the book *Twitter Tips, Tricks, and Tweets* by Paul McFedries. McFedries is a great writer, and he did an excellent job in creating a detailed, yet easy-to-follow, guide to all of Twitter's features and tools. Moreover, I am not the only person who recommends his book; so do the folks at Twitter. Check it out on Twitter's website at **http://business.twitter.com/twitter101/resources**.

Before we plunge into the how-to steps of using Twitter, I would like to offer some words of caution regarding what Twitter — and this chapter for that matter — is not about. This chapter will not recommend that you use Twitter to tell your followers in agonizing detail what you had for lunch today. This chapter will not recommend spending time on Twitter that is not 100 percent focused on your viral social networking goals, and you will not find any time-wasting, entertainment-oriented steps here. Plus, we will not use Twitter to follow the whereabouts of celebrities each day. Nor will we will be using Twitter to essentially "Retweet™" the daily news feed from within your industry because that requires no creativity or effort at all.

Lastly, we will not be sending an endless number of Tweets into the Tweeterverse in order to persuade your followers to buy your product or service. In *Twitter Tips, Tricks, and Tweets*, McFedries calls this form of activity "hypertweeting." Hypertweeting is defined as the "posting of an excessive number of Tweets." Based on my experience on determining the right number of Tweets to send each day, I think McFedries' hypertweeting definition is spot on. *Chapter 5 contains simple guidelines to follow that will help you avoid this common mistake.*

Search Engine Indexing of Tweets

There are a number of reasons why Twitter is effective at driving traffic to a website. One of the most fundamental reasons involves the indexing of your Tweets by Google and Bing-Yahoo!. Both of these search engines will index all of your Tweets. This makes the content within your Tweets searchable and valuable not only from a social networking perspective but also for search engine optimization. As a result, if you are strategic and include keywords within your Tweets and someone searches for those keywords within Google or Bing™ search engine, your Tweets may be displayed to the person within their Google or Bing search results.

For example, Figures 3.1 and 3.2 illustrate the search results on Google and Bing-Yahoo! for the keyword phrase "stephen woessner inc magazine." I searched this keyword phrase because I wanted to see if Google or Bing-Yahoo! had indexed a recent Tweet I made following an interview for an SEO-related story I completed with *Inc. Magazine*. As the following figures show, both Google and Bing-Yahoo! indexed the Tweet. I tested this theory further by searching the content of other Tweets, and each time, the Tweets had been indexed by Google and Bing-Yahoo!. In addition, the search results between Google and Bing-Yahoo! are nearly identical, which leads me to believe there could be some similarities in the process that both search engines use to index content.

Figure 3.1 Google's search results for a specific Tweet

©2010 Google

Figure 3.2 Bing's search results for a specific Tweet

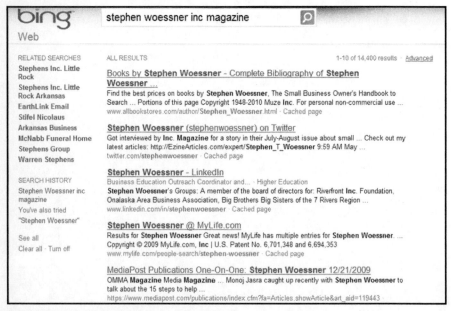

© 2010 Microsoft. Used with permission from Microsoft.

You may have noticed that in the previous paragraphs, I referred to Bing and Yahoo as "Bing-Yahoo!." As of August 24, 2010, Bing began powering all of the searches conducted on Yahoo!.

Creating a Twitter Account

Now, it is time for you to create your free account on Twitter, assuming you have not already done so. Begin by opening a Web browser, such as Internet Explorer, Mozilla Firefox, or Google Chrome, and go to Twitter's website (**http://twitter.com**). You will see a screen that looks similar to Figure 3.3 when you arrive at Twitter. Completing Twitter's account setup process is fast and efficient. In fact, it is by far the quickest of the three networks you will use as part of your viral social networking strategy.

Figure 3.3 Twitter welcome screen

© 2010 Twitter

In the upper right of Twitter's initial welcome screen, you will see a yellow "Sign Up" button. Click the "Sign Up" button, and you will be taken to Twitter's "Join the Conversation" page that will look similar to the one shown in Figure 3.4.

Figure 3.4 Twitter sign-up page

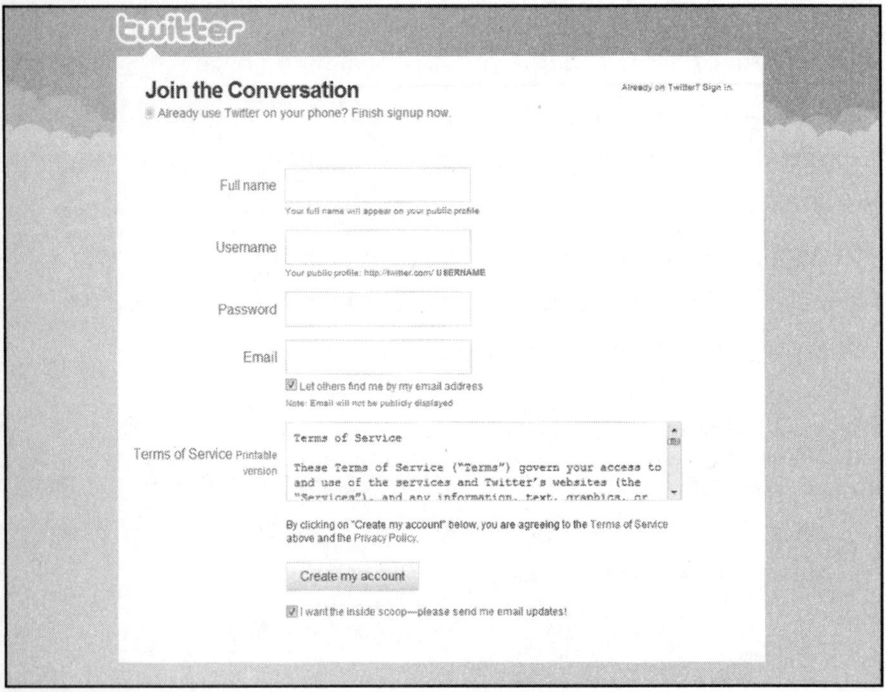

© 2010 Twitter

You simply need to fill in four pieces of information on this page: 1) your full name, 2) your desired Twitter username, 3) your desired Twitter password, and 4) your e-mail address. I recommend that you leave the default checked next to the box, "Let others find me by my e-mail address" because as your online community grows, you will likely have Facebook friends and LinkedIn connections search for you on Twitter via your e-mail address. Leaving this box checked will facilitate that process.

At the bottom of this page, you will notice there is another box that by default is checked. The box reads, "I want the inside scoop — please send me e-mail updates." My preference is it to typically uncheck these types of promotional boxes. I do this in an effort to limit the amount of nonessential e-mail I receive on a daily basis, but you might find Twitter's updates to be informative and valuable so do whatever you feel is appropriate for your situation.

Click the "Create my account" button once you have filled in the four pieces of information. You will then receive a verification screen similar to the one shown in Figure 3.5. The verification screen is used to determine that you are a real person versus a computer algorithm attempting to create fictitious Twitter accounts. Simply type the displayed words into the provided field, and then click the "Finish" button.

Figure 3.5 Twitter's human verification screen

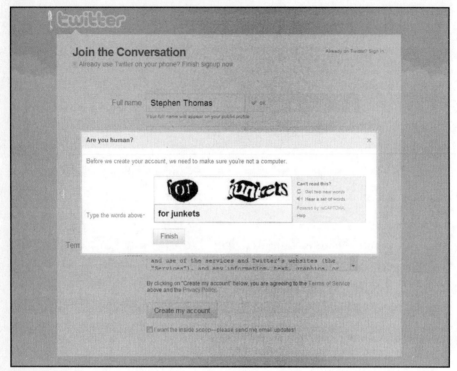

© 2010 Twitter

You are now close to completing the setup process. The next screen will look similar to the "Find sources that interest you" shown in Figure 3.6. From here, Twitter will help you find people you might be interested in following, as well as help you look up people you know via e-mail to see if they are already using Twitter.

Figure 3.6 Find people you want to follow

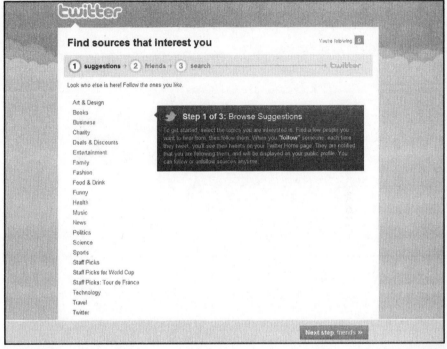

© 2010 Twitter

Step 1 in the process is the "Suggestions" feature. By clicking the categories on the left side of the screen, Twitter will display lists of well-known Tweeters who might be of interest to you. For this example, I clicked on the category "Business," which then provides a long list of popular businesspeople who actively use Twitter. To the right of each person or organization's name there is a gray "Follow" button. Simply click the "Follow" button, and you will begin receiving the Tweets that person or organization sends.

Click the blue "Next step: friends" button in the bottom right of the screen once you have finished selecting the people or organizations you would like to begin following immediately. You will then be taken to the second step in the process, which is shown in Figure 3.7.

Figure 3.7 Find friends already using Twitter

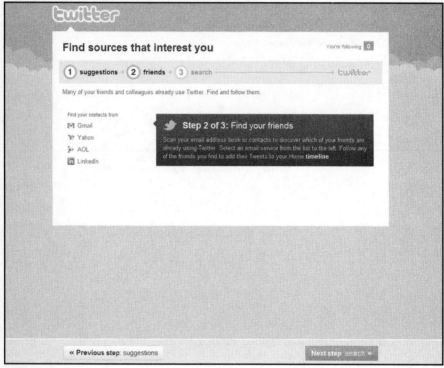

Twitter's "friends" tool will help you find friends who already use Twitter. This tool works very similar to the "Find Friends" feature you already used during Chapter 2 when you set up your Facebook account. LinkedIn also has a similar process to help you jumpstart the number of connections in your network.

To use this function on Twitter, roll your mouse over the e-mail service provider you currently use, which can be Gmail, Yahoo!, or AOL. For this example, we will assume you use Gmail for your e-mail. When you click on "Gmail," you will be asked to enter your Gmail username and password. When you do, Twitter will access and download your Gmail contact list. Twitter will then compare your Gmail contact lists with its database and provide you with a list of matches. You can then review the list and decide who you would like to follow via Twitter.

You can still find friends on Twitter via an e-mail address lookup even if you do not use Gmail, Yahoo!, or AOL as your e-mail client. For example, maybe you use Microsoft Outlook as your e-mail client. If this is your situation, simply click on the "Find On Twitter" tab, and type in a person's first and last name to search for him or her. The real downside to doing this is that it becomes a one-at-a-time type process and can consume a lot of time.

There is one more feature that needs to be discussed before we move on. Twitter now provides you with the ability to connect to your LinkedIn account via Twitter and follow any of your LinkedIn connections who also use Twitter.

Click on the LinkedIn logo from the menu on the left to begin the process of connecting your Twitter account with your LinkedIn account. You will receive a screen similar to the one shown in Figure 3.8. Do not worry if you do not have a LinkedIn account set up yet. You can come back to Twitter in the future and integrate your accounts at any time.

Figure 3.8 Connect your Twitter and LinkedIn accounts

© 2010 Twitter
LinkedIn Corporation © 2010

Now, click the blue "Go to LinkedIn" button at the bottom of the screen to continue the process. You will then receive a screen similar to the one shown in Figure 3.9. A few seconds may pass as the application works to establish the connection between your Twitter and LinkedIn accounts.

Figure 3.9 Application information via LinkedIn

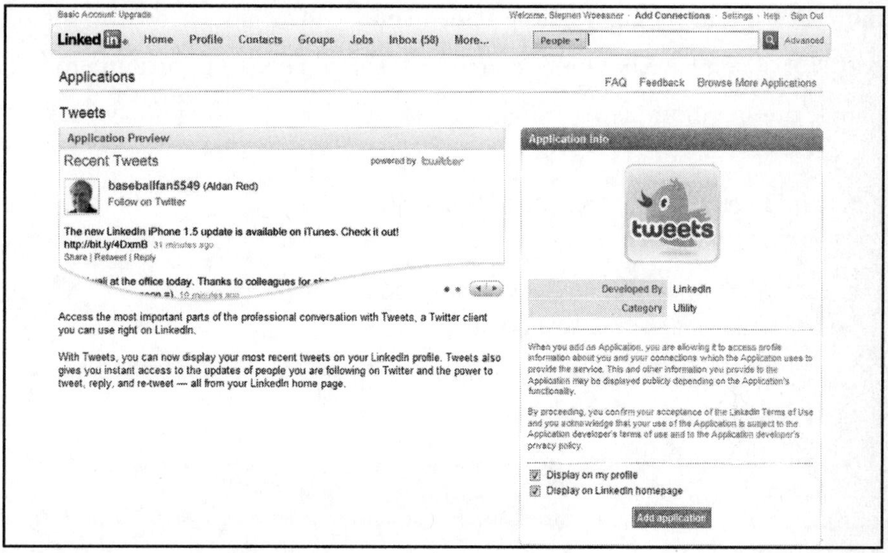

© 2010 Twitter
LinkedIn Corporation © 2010

Once the application loads, you will see a blue button in the bottom right that reads "Add application." Click this button, and LinkedIn will display a list of your LinkedIn network connections who also use Twitter. To the right of each person's name will be a Twitter "Follow" button. Simply click the button next to your LinkedIn connections who you want to also follow on Twitter. This is a powerful tool because many people who use Twitter have what is called an "auto-follow" feature enabled for their Twitter accounts. Auto-follow means that as soon as someone decides to follow them, they automatically begin following that person, too. So you will likely boost your number of Twitter followers by following your LinkedIn connections on Twitter because some of them are bound to use the auto-follow feature.

The final step in the process is the "search" function, which was actually described earlier as part of the "friends" discussion. If you already used the search function, simply skip it by clicking the blue "Next step: You're done!" button in the lower right of the screen similar to what is shown in Figure 3.10. Or, if you have not used "search" yet, this is a good opportunity to find people or organizations you might be interested in following on Twitter.

Figure 3.10 Congratulations...you're finished!

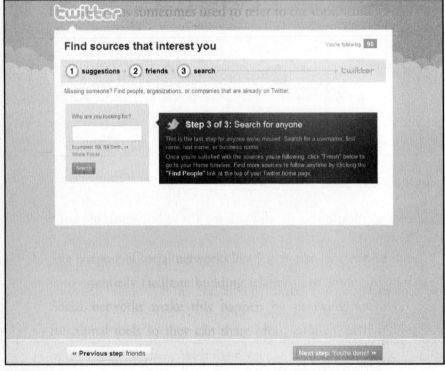

Customize Your Twitter Profile

You are now ready to customize your Twitter profile so people can learn more about you. Your profile will also help others find you, as people search for Tweeters they may be interested in following. This makes the content of your profile one of the most important tactics for recruiting more followers. Your profile will likely motivate a person to decide to follow you so think carefully about the content you decide to use. But, this content is also very easy to change so experimenting with what works best for you is no problem at all. Use the following steps to customize your Twitter profile:

1. Log in to your Twitter account.

2. Click the "Settings" link in the upper right corner of the Twitter menu in order to access the individual settings of your Twitter account.

3. Click on the "Profile" tab within the "Settings" menu, which is shown in Figure 3.11.

4. Click on the "Change image" link in order to replace the default image that Twitter provided you during the account setup process. I recommend that you use a photo similar to what you used as your Facebook profile photo in order to promote a consistent image for yourself.

5. Within the "Web" field, enter the address for the website to which you would like to refer traffic from Twitter.

6. Lastly, write a bio where you describe yourself in brief detail, as you are only allowed 160 characters. Your bio should contain

keywords that would likely match up with people who search for Tweeters to follow. For example, my Twitter bio reads, "SEO and social networking strategist, best-selling author, speaker, and small business expert."

7. Click the "Save" button, and you are finished with your Twitter profile.

Figure 3.11 Customize your profile settings

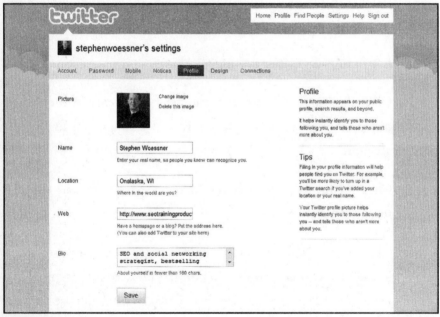

© 2010 Twitter

Select Your Background Image

The next step in the customizing process of your Twitter account is to select a background image. Twitter provides approximately 20 different design themes for you to consider. Each theme is fine and can be applied to your Twitter account in just a few clicks of your mouse. Click on the blue "Design" tab within your account settings menu, and you will be taken to a screen similar to the one shown in Figure 3.12. This screen will provide you with a visual list of the current templates that Twitter makes available to you.

The downside to using one of the themes provided by Twitter is that everyone who visits your Twitter profile will deduce that you are new to Twitter and perhaps just getting started.

Figure 3.12 Select your background image

© 2010 Twitter

I recommend you consider the following alternatives to make your Twitter background more visually appealing and professional:

▸ Experiment with using your own digital photos as your Twitter background. You can easily change the background image by clicking on the "Change background image" link at the bottom on the "Design" page shown in Figure 3.12.

▸ Visit the TwitBacks website (**www.twitbacks.com**), and consider using its free design service.

▸ Or, you can hire a graphic designer to create a JPEG layout you can upload as a background image. Typically, a professionally designed background image provides your Twitter followers with consistent branding to what they might experience on your business website. This is a terrific strategy, and I have seen it work very well for many Tweeters.

Begin Tweeting and Attracting Followers

Writing Tweets about topics of interest to your followers is one of the best ways to attract a steady flow of followers. The reason for this is two-fold: 1) The content of your Tweets is searchable within Twitter at **www.search. twitter.com** and 2) the content of your Tweets is indexed by Google, Bing, and other search engines, as discussed earlier in this chapter. *See Chapters 5 and 7 for practices to help guide you regarding the optimum number of Tweets a day you should write and the context of the content.*

The following steps can help you write your first Tweet and begin attracting followers:

1. Log in to your Twitter account.

2. Your cursor will begin flashing in the "What's happening?" field shown in Figure 3.13.

3. Type a message that is no more than 140 characters in length. You can also embed links into your Tweet. But, each character within the Web address link counts toward the 140 characters. You should consider using a free service such as TinyURL.com® (**http://tinyurl. com/**) or bit.ly® (**http://bit.ly/**) if you plan to embed a long link into your Tweet.

4. Consider placing a hashtag, which is the # sign directly in front of words you think would be keywords used by people who may search for topics of interest on Twitter. For example, say I am writing a Tweet about search engine optimization. I might use the following: *I am thrilled that my #SEO book has become an Amazon.com best-seller in the United States, UK, and France!* This Tweet used 106 characters of the 140-character limit, and I placed a hashtag in front of SEO, a potential keyword.

5. Click the gray "Tweet" button beneath the "What's happening?" field when you have finished writing your message.

Figure 3.13 Writing your first Tweet

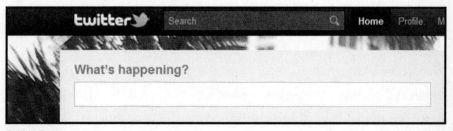

© 2010 Twitter

This section of the chapter would not be complete without some words of caution. Please use caution if you find yourself considering the claims of third-party services that promise they can quickly provide you with a large number of followers in exchange for a one-time or monthly subscription fee. This type of promise is delivered via spam activities, such as follower trains, selling usernames, and phishing. You want a follower list that is highly targeted toward you and your profile. Paying a third-party service to build a list of followers that consist of people who have never heard of you, or even worse, are not even familiar with the subject you represent is a complete waste of time and money.

Twitter does not permit this type of fast follower acquisition activity. Visit Twitter's website at **http://support.twitter.com/articles/68916-following-rules-and-best-practices** for a more detailed explanation from Twitter.

Replies and Retweets

When I first started using Twitter, the network really felt like a one-way conversation. I would write and post Tweets, and they would be sent off into the Twitterverse and never be heard from again. And then one day, I Tweeted about a new article I had written and posted on my website. The article discussed several best practice SEO techniques business owners could use to increase their search engine rankings on Google. None of the techniques in the article were controversial; however, one of my Twitter followers adamantly disagreed with the recommendations I had offered.

The follower disagreed so much that the person "replied" to my original Tweet and criticized the methods I had recommended. Replying to a Tweet is simply the process of responding to the original Tweeter. But, replies become public conversation. Replies are not private messages like Twitter's direct message feature. Therefore, you want to use discretion when replying because thousands of people may read what you write.

I was not offended by the reply in the least. Instead, the reply I received was an excellent opportunity to banter back and forth via a series of replies to address this person's concerns. In the end, the reply was an efficient method to address the person's concerns.

Use the following steps to reply to the Tweet of someone you follow:

1. Log in to your Twitter account, and click on the "Home" tab.

2. From your home page you will see all of the most recent Tweets for all of the people you follow in your account.

3. Find a Tweet to which you would like to write a reply.

4. Roll your mouse over the Tweet, and you will see the "Reply" and "Retweet" links directly below the Tweet, as shown in Figure 3.14.

5. Click on the "Reply" link.

6. Twitter will display a pop-up window in the center of your screen with the pre-populated address of the person to whom you are replying. All you have to do is write your reply, as show in Figure 3.15.

7. Click the gray "Tweet" button once you have finished writing your reply.

8. Your reply will automatically become the next Tweet posted on your Twitter home page for your followers to read.

Figure 3.14 Replying to someone else's Tweet

Figure 3.15 Replying to someone else's Tweet

Retweets

Retweet describes the process of copying another person's Tweet and sending it out to your followers. Twitter automatically includes an acknowledgment of the original Tweeter. Retweeting is a great tool for passing along a topic you feel should be shared with your followers because it has value to others.

Retweets you distribute will not show up on your Twitter home page like a reply to a Tweet. Instead, your Retweets are only visible on the Twitter pages of the people who follow you. Figure 3.16 illustrates this point.

For example, DessertGallery is the Twitter name of a company that I follow. Dessert Gallery posted a Tweet that read, "stop by dessertgallery come watch The Santa Clause and then at 7 Texans vs Eagles dessertgallery at Kirby bring the family or friends." The Tweet is shown Figure 3.16. I decided to Retweet this message to all of my Twitter followers so I rolled my mouse over the Tweet, and Twitter displayed the "Retweet" link below the original Tweet. If the "Retweet" link is clicked, Twitter will provide you with a screen that looks similar to Figure 3.17.

Figure 3.16 Dessert Gallery Tweet

© 2010 Twitter

Figure 3.17 Retweeting the Dessert Gallery Tweet

© 2010 Twitter

Click the blue "Retweet" button shown in the screen shot, and you are finished with the Retweeting process. Retweeting is similar to replying, but it is much faster because you do not have to write a reply message. Use the following steps to Retweet a Tweet to you followers:

1. Log in to your Twitter account, and click on the "Home" tab.

2. From your home page, you will see the most recent Tweets of the people you follow.

3. Find a Tweet you would like to Retweet.

4. Roll your mouse over the Tweet, and you will see the "Reply" and "Retweet" links directly below the Tweet, as shown in Figure 3.14.

5. Click on the "Retweet" link.

6. When you see the "Retweet to your followers?" message appear, simply click the gray "Yes" button.

7. Twitter will then distribute the Retweet to all of your followers with an acknowledgement to the original Tweeter.

8. The Retweeted message will then become visible on your Twitter "Home" tab, as shown in Figure 3.18.

Figure 3.18 Confirms your Retweet

I mentioned earlier that one of the phenomena about Twitter is that people tend to Tweet on the go using their mobile phones. Therefore, I recommend that you consider learning how to download, install, and use the Twitter application designed for use on your mobile phone. Chapter 5 in Paul McFedries's book *Twitter Tips, Tricks, and Tweets* covers the process in specific detail. Using Twitter via a mobile phone is not complicated, but I decided not to cover it in this chapter because I do not consider it a critical element to your viral social networking success.

Viral Social Networking Checklist: Part 3

❏ Sign up for your free Twitter account.

❏ Find and begin following people or companies that interest you by using Twitter's "Find sources that interest you" feature.

❏ Find and follow your friends who already use Twitter by uploading your e-mail contacts folder similar to the process you followed with Facebook in Chapter 2.

❏ Connect your Twitter and LinkedIn accounts so you can begin following any of your LinkedIn connections via Twitter, assuming those people have Twitter accounts.

❏ Customize your Twitter profile photo, bio, website address, and geographic location.

❏ Customize your Twitter Home page background with a graphic, photo, or other template.

❏ Write and post your first Tweet, and begin attracting followers.

❏ Begin replying to Tweets posted by a person or company you follow.

❏ Begin Retweeting the Tweets posted by a person or company you follow.

❏ Proceed to Chapter 4: LinkedIn Fundamentals.

CHAPTER 4:

LinkedIn Fundamentals

Viral social networking steps covered in this chapter:

▸ Step 4: Get started with LinkedIn.

Establishing a foundation with Facebook and Twitter was the purpose of Chapters 2 and 3. The same is true with Chapter 4. This chapter will provide you with the essentials you need to begin using LinkedIn as part of your viral social networking strategy.

As you read and study this chapter, please keep the following statement in mind: The profile you create on LinkedIn will essentially serve as your professional Web page similar to an online résumé or a professional advertisement for you. Your LinkedIn profile should be designed with the purpose of promoting you, your experience, and the value you can deliver to your clients or customers.

Before we get started with the how-to steps in creating your LinkedIn profile, we should review some terminology differences between Facebook,

Twitter, and LinkedIn. The people who join your Facebook community are called "friends," and within Twitter they are called "followers." Within the LinkedIn network, these people are called "connections." In addition, in Facebook you will write "status updates," and on Twitter you write "Tweets" to communicate with your community members. You will write "network updates" within LinkedIn.

Creating a LinkedIn Account

It is time for you to create your free account on LinkedIn, assuming you have not already done so. Begin by opening a Web browser, such as Internet Explorer, Mozilla Firefox, or Google Chrome, and go to LinkedIn's website (**www.linkedin.com**). You will see a screen that looks similar to Figure 4.1 when you arrive at LinkedIn.

Figure 4.1 LinkedIn welcome screen

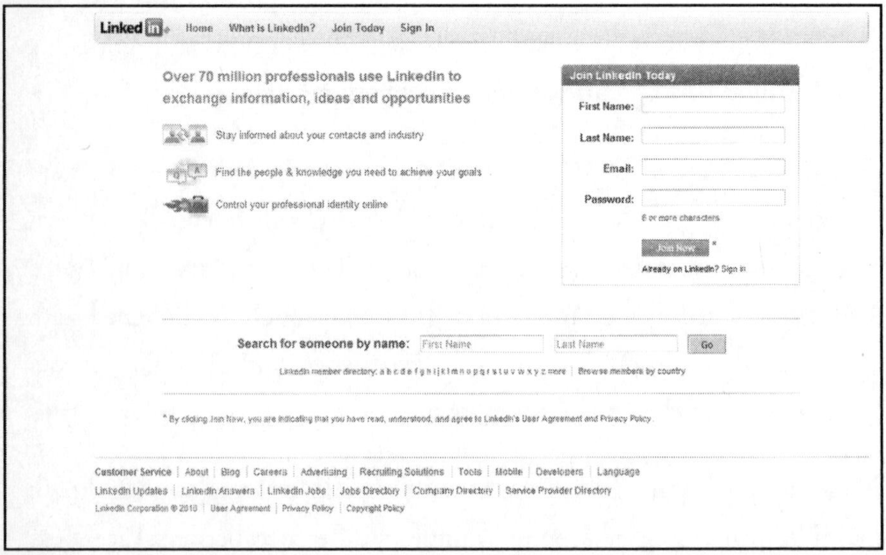

LinkedIn Corporation © 2010

In the upper right corner of the LinkedIn screen, you will see a blue bar that reads "Join LinkedIn Today," which is also shown in Figure 4.2. All you need to do to create your initial account is to enter your first and last name, your e-mail address, and a desired password into the fields provided. Then, click the green "Join Now" button once you have entered the information.

Figure 4.2 LinkedIn's signup screen

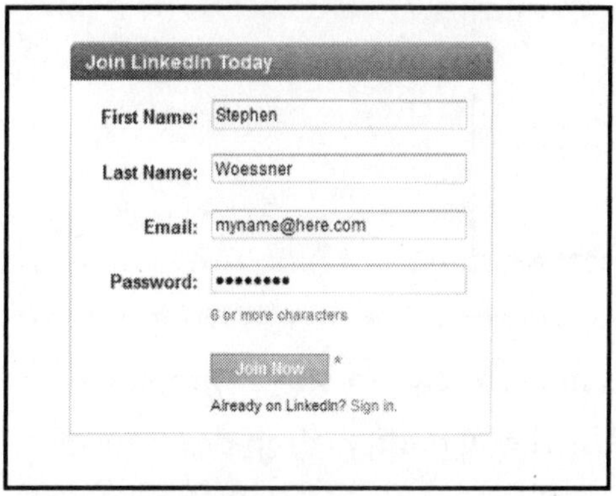

LinkedIn Corporation © 2010

You will then be taken to a LinkedIn screen that looks similar to the screen shot displayed in Figure 4.3. It is on this screen that LinkedIn begins collecting some of the information it needs to create your professional profile. Even though it is not labeled as such, this screen is the first of six steps in LinkedIn's initial account creation process.

Figure 4.3 LinkedIn collects basic information

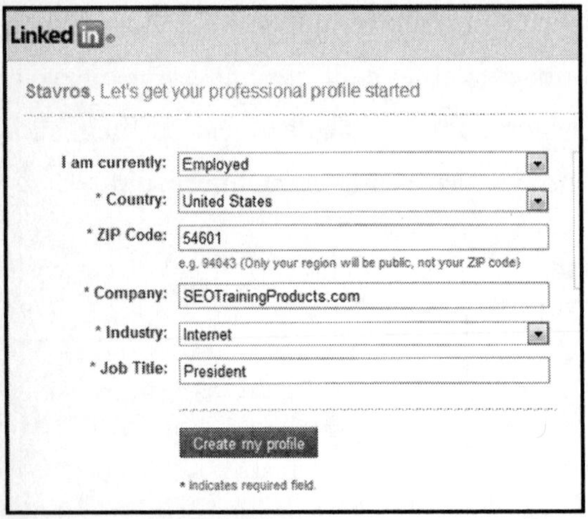

LinkedIn Corporation © 2010

Use the drop-down menu titled "I am currently" to select "Employed" or one of the other available options. Use the "Country" drop-down menu to select the country in which you live. Then, enter your ZIP code into the field provided. If you are currently employed, LinkedIn will require you to enter the name of your company, select the industry that your company serves, and provide your job title. Once you have entered all of the required information on this screen, click the blue "Create my profile" button.

You will then be taken to a screen similar to what is shown in Figure 4.4. From this screen, you can allow LinkedIn to search your e-mail contacts to find people you know who are already LinkedIn members. This step in the process is very similar to the steps you completed while creating your Facebook and Twitter accounts. You can also choose to "Skip this step" by clicking the link in the lower right of the screen. You can always search your e-mail contacts at a later date if you choose so do not worry if you prefer to skip it now.

Figure 4.4 Find people you already know who use LinkedIn

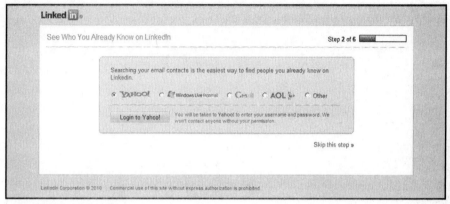

LinkedIn Corporation © 2010

If you decide to skip it, you will receive a screen similar to what is shown in Figure 4.5. This informs you that LinkedIn has sent a verification e-mail to the e-mail address you provided. You will need to access your e-mail account, open the e-mail from LinkedIn, and click on the link within the e-mail before you can complete the LinkedIn account setup process.

Figure 4.5 Confirm your e-mail address

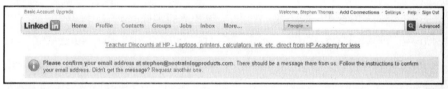

LinkedIn Corporation © 2010

You will be taken to a screen that looks similar to Figure 4.6 after you click the verification link found in your e-mail.

Figure 4.6 Invite people to join you on LinkedIn

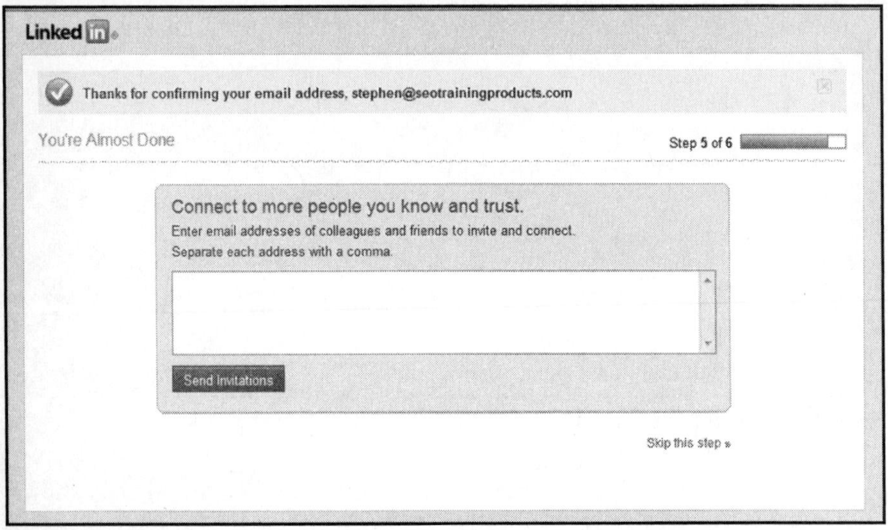

LinkedIn Corporation © 2010

During the next step in signup process, you can enter the e-mail addresses of colleagues and friends who you want LinkedIn to extend an invitation to join you on LinkedIn. This step is only for inviting people you know to join LinkedIn. In my opinion, I tend not to use social networking features like this because I have heard negative comments in the workplace from people who were invited to join a social network by someone they knew and the invitation was met with skepticism or was seen as intrusive. With that said, feel free to use this feature if you are so inclined. Ultimately, you will likely see a low number of colleagues and friends who actually create LinkedIn accounts in order to connect with you. Please do not be offended if this is the case. From what I have observed, people can easily feel pressured to join a social network, and this is obviously counterproductive from the positive relationships you are attempting to create.

Once you complete this step, or if you decide to skip it, you will receive a screen similar to what is shown in Figure 4.7. This is where LinkedIn asks if you would like to upgrade to a Premium account versus the Basic (free) account.

Figure 4.7 Select your preferred account level

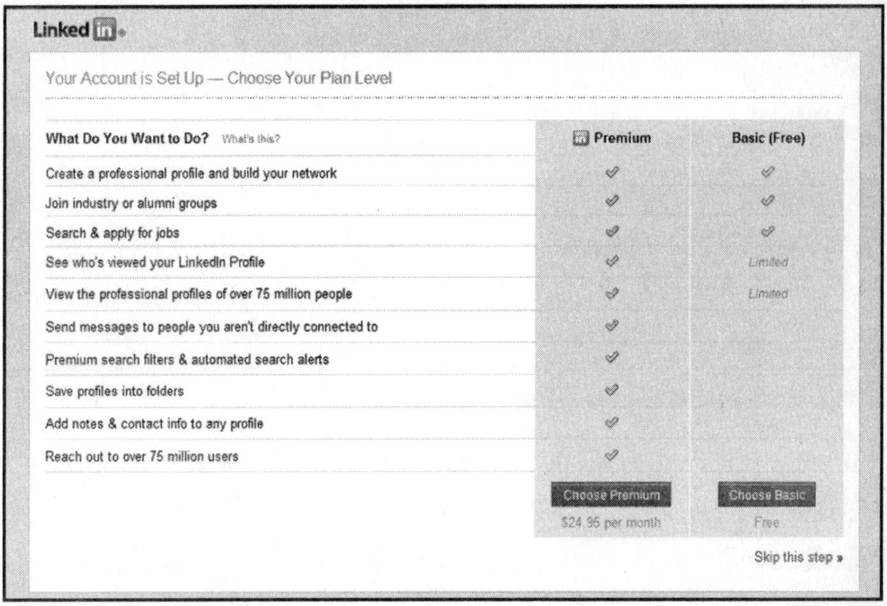

LinkedIn Corporation © 2010

In my experience, as well as from listening to feedback from other LinkedIn members, I have never heard from anyone who has felt that having a premium LinkedIn account was critical to the success of his or her social networking strategy. Regardless, you should review the list of available features for LinkedIn's Premium and basic accounts so you can decide which account level is the best fit for your needs. Assuming you decide to remain at the Basic level, click the blue "Choose Basic" button in the bottom right of the screen shown in Figure 4.7.

You will know that your initial LinkedIn account creation process has been completed when you receive a screen that looks similar to Figure 4.8.

Figure 4.8 LinkedIn confirms account creation

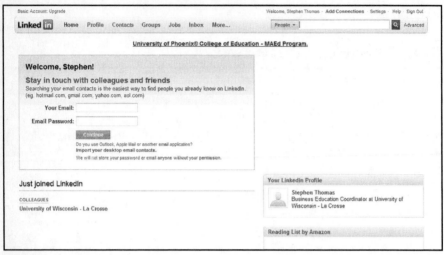

LinkedIn Corporation © 2010

This screen welcomes you in the upper left with the "Welcome, Stephen!" message. You can also see the beginning of your professional profile in the lower left and right corners of this screen. The lower left corner provides a link that will help you find colleagues at your current place of employment who already use LinkedIn. With respect to the initial profile in this example, LinkedIn is providing me with a link to find colleagues who also work at the University of Wisconsin-La Crosse. LinkedIn uses the lower right corner to display the content that it collected from you during the account creation process, such as current occupation.

Finding LinkedIn Connections

Do not worry if you chose not to provide LinkedIn with permission to search your e-mail contacts during the account creation process because you can do that at any time by clicking the green "Add Connections" link in the upper right of your screen. When you click the "Add Connections" link, you will receive a screen that looks similar to what is displayed in Figure 4.9.

Figure 4.9 Find more LinkedIn connections

LinkedIn Corporation © 2010

From this screen, you can provide LinkedIn with the permission to search your e-mail contacts, or you can chose to enter e-mail addresses of people you would like LinkedIn to send invitations to on your behalf to join you on LinkedIn.

However, LinkedIn also provides some other useful features from this screen that are particularly helpful once you complete your profile. For example, to the right of the "Add Connections" tab, you will see three additional tabs for "Colleagues," "Classmates," and "People You May Know." The colleagues and classmates functions are relatively straightforward. For example, you will be able to find other LinkedIn members who listed the same places of employment as you when they created their own profiles. You can then decide whether to send each of your colleagues an individual invitation to connect via LinkedIn. LinkedIn does not send bulk invitations.

Within the "People You May Know" section, LinkedIn looks for potential relationships by reviewing your current list of connections in order to find other LinkedIn members who share connections with you. LinkedIn will display the photo, occupation, and the number of shared connections for each person that it determines could be a relevant connection for you. You can then decide whether to invite these people to become connections.

You need to be aware that LinkedIn only allows basic members to send and/or accept a maximum of 3,000 invitations to connections. This is likely an ample number of connections for most LinkedIn users, but you should know that this constraint exists.

Completing Your LinkedIn Profile

Now, it is time to create and edit your LinkedIn profile, which essentially consists of eight primary content elements or sections:

1. Your photo
2. Current employment
3. Past employment
4. Education
5. Recommendations
6. Link to websites
7. Link to Twitter account
8. Your professional summary

Completing these sections is like using your existing résumé to copy sections into LinkedIn's predetermined fields. The most time consuming part of creating your LinkedIn profile will be writing the professional summary, unless you already have one prepared. If you do, you can simply copy and paste it into your profile. Your completed profile will look similar to Figure

4.10. Feel free to visit the online version of my LinkedIn profile at **www. linkedin.com/in/stephenwoessner** if you would like to review a tangible example while developing your own profile.

Figure 4.10 Completing your LinkedIn profile

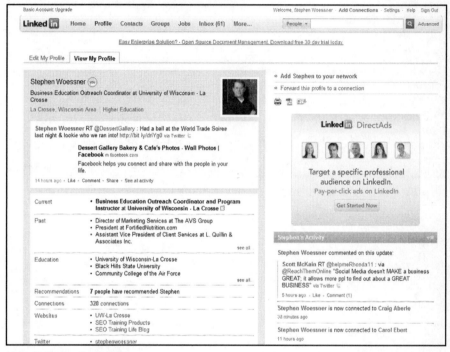

LinkedIn Corporation © 2010

To access your profile within LinkedIn, simply roll your mouse over the "Profile" tab within the LinkedIn menu near the top of your browser window. You will be able to select either the "Edit Profile" or "View Profile" options, as shown in Figure 4.11. Both options will give you access to your full profile, but only the edit option will provide you with an editable version.

Figure 4.11 Accessing your LinkedIn profile

LinkedIn Corporation © 2010

The beginning version of your editable version of your profile will look similar to the screen shot shown in Figure 4.12. Each of the content sections will initially be empty and can be accessed and edited by clicking the small blue "Add" links next to each section.

Figure 4.12 Editable sections of your profile

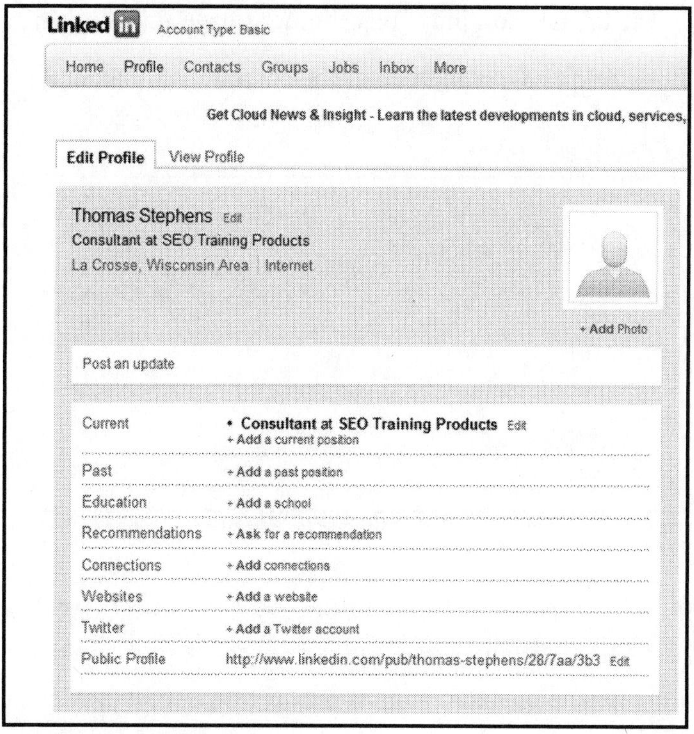

Linked **in**   Account Type: Basic

| Home | Profile | Contacts | Groups | Jobs | Inbox | More |

Get Cloud News & Insight - Learn the latest developments in cloud, services,

Edit Profile   View Profile

Thomas Stephens   Edit
Consultant at SEO Training Products
La Crosse, Wisconsin Area | Internet

+ Add Photo

Post an update

Current	• **Consultant at SEO Training Products** Edit + Add a current position
Past	+ Add a past position
Education	+ Add a school
Recommendations	+ Ask for a recommendation
Connections	+ Add connections
Websites	+ Add a website
Twitter	+ Add a Twitter account
Public Profile	http://www.linkedin.com/pub/thomas-stephens/28/7aa/3b3 Edit

LinkedIn Corporation © 2010

Your photo

The first content section you can quickly check off your list is the addition of a professional photo. I recommend that you keep the process simple by using the same photo from your Facebook and Twitter profiles. Using the same photo also presents a consistent visual message to all of the members of your online brand community who happen to be your Facebook friend, Twitter follower, and LinkedIn connection.

You will receive a screen similar to Figure 4.13 when you click the blue "Add Photo" link next to the temporary placeholder image that LinkedIn provided you during the account creation process.

Figure 4.13 Updating your profile photo

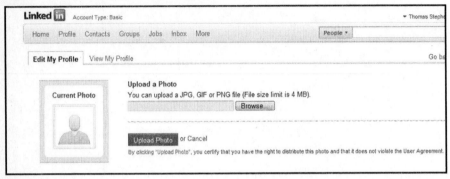

LinkedIn Corporation © 2010

Click the gray "Browse" button to find the photo on your hard drive you would like to upload. Then, click the blue "Upload Photo" button. LinkedIn will then upload the photo. Once the photo uploads, LinkedIn will ask you to specify with whom you would like to share your photo. For example, you will have several options: 1) My connections, 2) My network, or 3) Everyone. As the name implies, the "My connections" selection will ensure your photo will only be visible by your specific connections. The "My network" selection will allow your photo to be shared with your connections, as well as the connections of your connections, which is obviously a broader audience. The third selection of "Everyone" is exactly as it sounds…anyone viewing your profile can view your photo. I recommend that you select "Everyone" so your photo has the greatest distribution possible. "Everyone" is also the default setting.

The remaining content sections, i.e. employment, etc., are relatively self-explanatory and easy to edit. Again, these sections can be copied and pasted from your résumé into the fields that LinkedIn provides, but the next major content section of your profile that does deserve attention is the summary.

Summary

You will receive a screen similar to Figure 4.14 when you click on the blue "Add Summary" link below your Summary section. Your summary consists of two main areas: 1) Professional Experience & Goals and 2) Specialties. From my experience in working with small business owners for nearly two decades, I have consistently witnessed a tendency to glaze over all of the details about our experiences and what we are really good at. Then, we are surprised when a client or customer does not select us for a certain project because he or she was unaware that we could have provided the necessary product or service — and perhaps for a better price. The client did not think to ask us because we did not proactively share a comprehensive overview of all we can do.

Figure 4.14 Add your professional summary

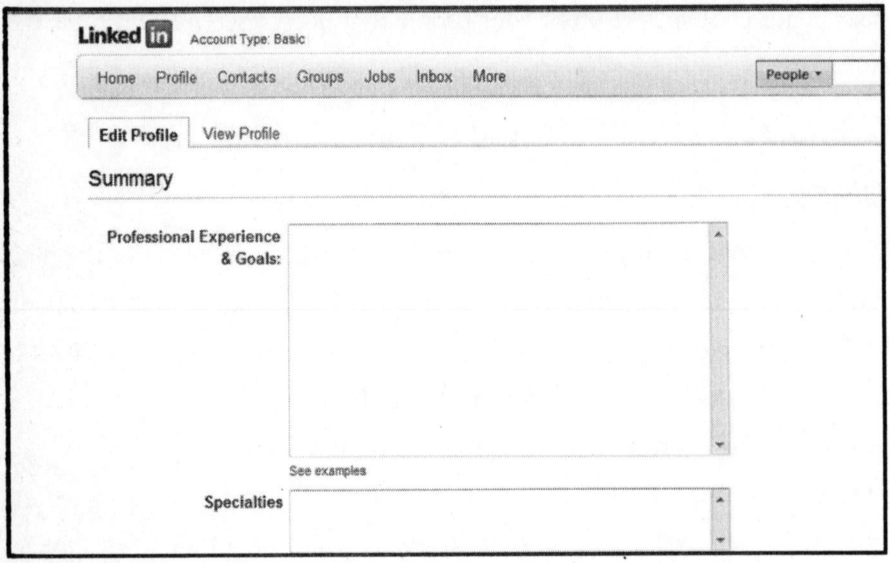

LinkedIn Corporation © 2010

I would never recommend that you brag or overextend your expertise. Instead, you should write a detailed, accurate, and humble summary of your capabilities and experience. The only constraint that LinkedIn puts on you is your summary must be 2,000 characters or less.

Then, click the blue "Save Changes" button when you finish writing your summary. LinkedIn will then upload your summary and combine it with the rest of your profile. Your profile will then be available to all of your connections.

Recommendations

Your LinkedIn profile will remain only partially complete until you collect at least three "recommendations" from your connections. Recommendations on LinkedIn are essentially testimonials from your colleagues and friends with whom you have had business dealings or some sort of professional relationship. You can collect recommendations regarding your role at your current place of employment, as well as each of your past places of employment. Each of the recommendations added to your LinkedIn profile, assuming the recommendation is positive, will enhance your professional credibility. The comments and examples shared by others are much more believable than anything you could ever write or say about yourself.

As shown in the aforementioned Figure 4.11, when you roll your mouse over "Profile" in the LinkedIn menu, "Recommendations" was the third of the four options. Click "Recommendations." When you do, you should see a screen similar to the screen shot shown in Figure 4.15. This screen will give you the ability to manage all of your LinkedIn recommendations, as well as request new recommendations from your connections.

Figure 4.15 Managing recommendations

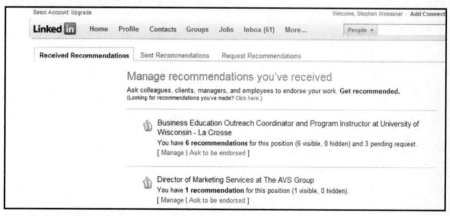

The process of adding recommendations to your profile begins by inviting your clients, colleagues, or other connections within your LinkedIn network to endorse you by writing a recommendation for you. You accomplish this by clicking the blue "Ask to be endorsed" link found under each of the places of employment for which you would like to receive a recommendation regarding the work you performed while employed at that company. Each of the places of employment you listed when creating your profile will have the this feature available.

When you click the link, you will receive a screen similar to what is shown in Figure 4.16. In Step 1, you select the place of employment for which you are seeking recommendations. In Step 2, you can manually type in the name(s) of the client(s) or colleague(s) to whom you would like LinkedIn to send an invitation to write a recommendation. Or, perhaps you work with a large number of clients in your current role or previous employer and many of them have become your LinkedIn connections. If so, you might want to click the small blue LinkedIn logo to the right of the empty field in Step 2. By doing so, you can quickly click the names of your connections from an alphabetized list generated by LinkedIn. When you are finished, LinkedIn will send this invitation regarding your work at the company you specified to as many as 200 of your connections all at once.

Figure 4.16 Recommendations request form

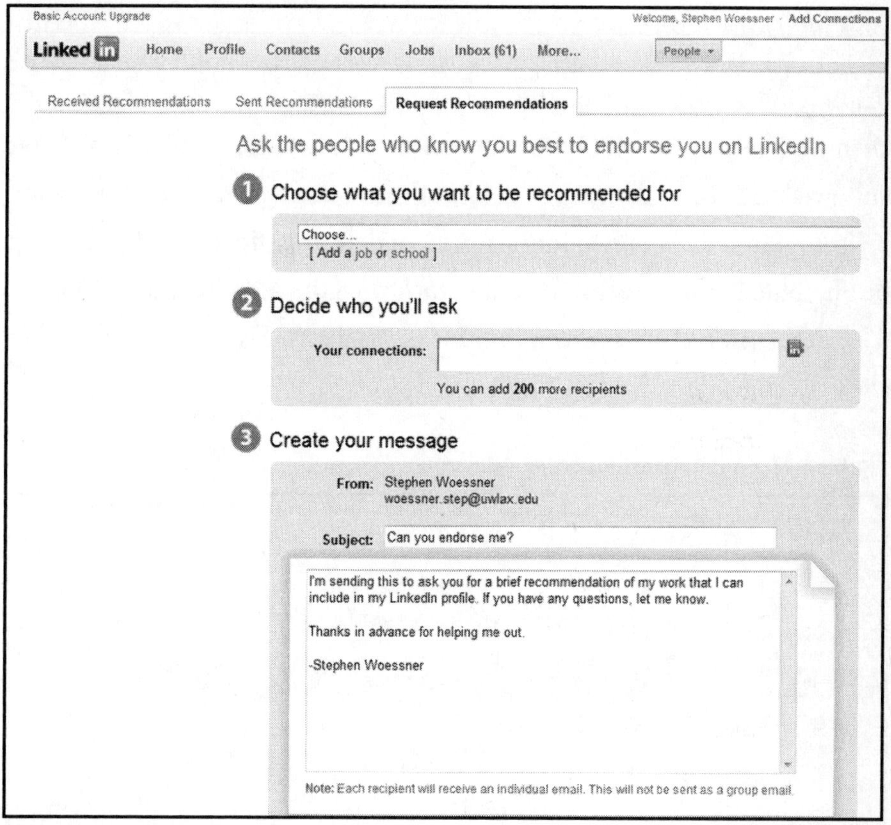

LinkedIn Corporation © 2010

Once you have created the list of recipients for your invitation, it is time to move on to Step 3 in the process. If you like, Step 3 gives you the opportunity to create a customized message within the invitation, but you can also choose to use the standard text that LinkedIn provides.

When you are finished with the messaging in Step 3, click the blue "Send" button at the bottom of the screen. LinkedIn will then send your invitations, and you will begin receiving recommendations. Do not be surprised if you receive recommendations relatively quickly. It will likely only take a couple of days for you to receive the necessary three recommendations to complete your profile.

Just so you know, none of the recommendations you receive from your clients or colleagues will be viewable unless you decide it is acceptable. You will need to specifically approve each of the recommendations for viewing by your LinkedIn connections. You complete this final step by clicking on the blue "Manage" link that was shown in the aforementioned Figure 4.15. You will receive a screen that looks similar to Figure 4.17 when you click the link.

Figure 4.17 Manage your recommendations

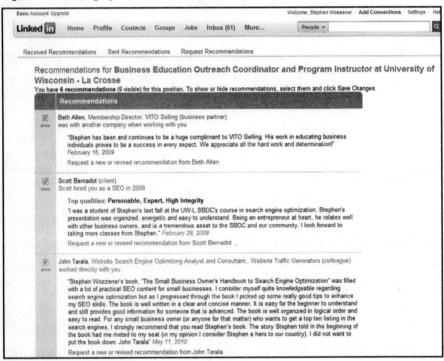

LinkedIn Corporation © 2010

LinkedIn will categorize all of the recommendations you have received by your employment history. Figure 4.17 represents a sampling of several of the recommendations I received regarding my role at the University of Wisconsin-La Crosse. To the left of each recommendation, you will see a box marked "Show." I have checked all three of the recommendations that are displayed. By checking the box, I gave LinkedIn permission to show all of my connections each recommendation.

But, if you happen to disagree with what a client or colleague wrote about your role at that company, you can follow up with that person by clicking the blue "Request a new or revised recommendation from…" link that LinkedIn places underneath each of your recommendations.

Lastly, when you receive and approve a recommendation from someone, LinkedIn will automatically invite you to return the favor by writing a recommendation for the person who just did it for you. This reciprocation is completely voluntary and does not affect your ability to post the recommendation you just received from that client or colleague. I always make the effort to return the favor. I consider it to be good business to do the same for someone who was already gracious enough to help you.

Overall, LinkedIn makes the process of requesting, approving, and managing your recommendations efficient and effective.

LinkedIn Account and Privacy Settings

In my opinion, the account and privacy settings available to you within your LinkedIn account are the most abundant of any of the three social networks covered in this book. LinkedIn provides you with an abundance of setting options in eight main categories: 1) Profile Settings, 2) E-mail Notifications,

3) Home Page Settings, 4) RSS Settings, 5) Groups, 6) Personal Information, 7) Privacy Settings, and 8) My Network, as shown in Figure 4.18.

You can access your LinkedIn account and privacy settings by clicking your first and last name, which LinkedIn displays in the upper right of the screen. When you do, a drop-down menu appears that contains two options: 1) Settings and 2) Sign Out. Click the Settings link.

During Chapter 2 within the privacy discussion as it related to Facebook, I shared that my goal has been to build as robust of an online brand community as possible. However, I still set my Facebook privacy settings to "Only Friends." I did this so I could be somewhat assured that I have a reasonable level of relationship with the people who have access to the content I post. Determining privacy settings is and has to remain a very personal decision. What I have decided is appropriate for me might not be appropriate for another user. As was the case with Facebook and Twitter, whatever you decide for your LinkedIn settings, all of the information in your profile, as well as the settings, can be updated and revised in the future no matter what you select at this early stage in building your profile.

Figure 4.18 Manage your account settings

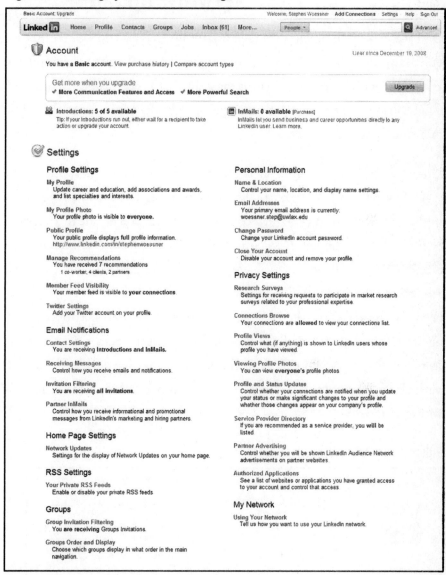

LinkedIn Corporation © 2010

Writing Your First Network Update

On Facebook, your updates are called status updates and on Twitter they are called Tweets. Within LinkedIn, your updates are called network updates, and the process of writing them is very similar. You can find the network update field on your LinkedIn home page, and it looks similar to the screen shot shown in Figure 4.19.

LinkedIn and Twitter have created a helpful feature into the network update that allows you to Tweet your LinkedIn network update as soon as you click the blue "Share" button — and vice versa. Whatever you decide to Tweet will be posted to your LinkedIn account. I really like this feature; although, there is one constraint. If you write a network update on LinkedIn and it exceeds 140 characters in length, Twitter will only post the first 140 characters so brevity is the key. But, you might prefer to only share short network updates on Twitter and always post the longer, more robust updates on LinkedIn. In that case, you would simply uncheck the Twitter box located to the left of the blue "Share" button. This will keep your network updates exclusively within LinkedIn.

Figure 4.19 Writing network updates

Network Activity

Share an update

Attach a link

Share

15 hours ago · RT @DessertGallery: Had a bal... · via Twitter · Comment · More »

LinkedIn Corporation © 2010

I will use one of my most recent network updates to illustrate the process of writing your first update. When my first book, *The Small Business Owner's*

Handbook to Search Engine Optimization was released, I quickly began getting e-mails from readers outside the United States. They had purchased the book, liked the 15 steps, and wanted to know if I was planning an international version as a future edition. I was shocked and then realized that I had made a very significant error when writing the book by not addressing important topics like Baidu® versus Google in China or search engines that must be factored into an SEO strategy within the United Kingdom, Germany, or other European Union countries. As a result, I recently wrote the following network update on LinkedIn: "Got a request to discuss Baidu vs. Google in China as part of an international version of my SEO book. And my book is being sold in Japan!"

To supplement the text, I wanted to include a link to where someone could find the book on the Amazon.com Japan website. Adding supporting links provides credibility to what you write in the update, and it will also give you the ability to drive traffic to your website and increase online sales. But, sometimes the links you want to share are very long and cumbersome. For example, the original version of the Amazon Japan link looked like this:

http://www.amazon.co.jp/Business-Owners-Handbook-Optimizatio n-Traffic/dp/1601384432/ref=sr_1_1?ie=UTF8&s=english-books&q id=128330...4607&sr=8-1

It would be advantageous for you to shorten the link, especially since Twitter will only post 140 characters, which includes the characters within the link. There are several free link shortening services online that provide a great solution to this problem. My favorite is TinyURL.com. Simply go to the company's website (**http://tinyurl.com**), paste in the link you want to shorten, click the gray "Make TinyURL" button to the right of the link you just pasted into the field, and TinyURL.com will immediately display the shortened link. In this case, TinyURL.com took my long Amazon.com Japan link and gave me the new link **http://tinyurl.com/2fwsc3q**.

The final step was to combine the text and the shortened link into a network update. Once I wrote the text into the network update field, I clicked the blue "Attach a link" link that LinkedIn provides underneath the text window. LinkedIn then provides an additional window so I could paste in the shortened URL. Once pasted, I clicked the blue "Attach" button. LinkedIn then finds the website referenced in the link and grabs several graphics from the site. As shown in Figure 4.20, LinkedIn grabbed the cover of my book from Amazon.com's website and gave me the choice of whether I would like to include a graphic as part of the update.

Figure 4.20 Adding links to a network update

LinkedIn Corporation © 2010

There is only one additional step I need to consider before clicking the blue "Share" button. I need to decide who I want to share the network update with. I can change who can view my network update at the bottom of the update box, as shown in Figure 4.20. Look for the phrase "Visible to." The default setting is "Anyone." However, you can choose to share your network update with only your connections if you prefer by click on the arrow. I typically leave the default setting of anyone.

Once done, I clicked the "Share" button, and LinkedIn distributed my update throughout my network of connections, as well as throughout the Twitterverse.

Commenting On Network Updates by Connections

You can comment on the network updates that any of your LinkedIn connections post. The commenting process works very similar to writing a comment on one of your Facebook friend's status updates or other content within Facebook. As I mentioned in Chapter 2, commenting on the updates posted by members of your online brand community is one of the best ways to develop conversation, which will ultimately lead to commerce.

Figure 4.21 shows the LinkedIn profile of a good friend of mine, Ted Stein. Ted owns a company called Stein Counseling and Consulting, which is the leading resource of experts serving individuals, families, and communities throughout southwest Wisconsin. You can find him at **www.effectivebehavior.com**. In Figure 4.21, you can see the network update that he wrote that reads, "Vote to give this idea 250k. Build a 'Comprehensive Youth Center' in La Crosse, WI for at-risk youth." He also included a link to the Pepsi Refresh Project voting website so people could vote on the proposal his company submitted in support of our community.

Figure 4.21 Viewing network updates of your connections

I decided I wanted to post a comment regarding his network update. Again, the process works the same as it does on Facebook. I simply clicked the blue "Comment" link beneath the network update. When the link was clicked, LinkedIn provided me with a comment window as shown in Figure 4.22. Then, I typed my comment that read, "This is an awesome project!" Then, I clicked the blue "Add Comment" button to post my comment.

Figure 4.22 Commenting on a connection's network update

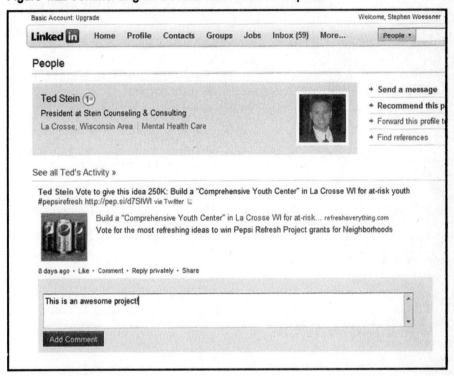

LinkedIn Corporation © 2010

Ted could also choose to respond to me by writing a comment regarding the message I posted. He would simply click on the blue "Comment" link directly under my comment, write a response, and click the blue "Add Comment" button. His comment would be posted directly below my comment.

The benefit to posting comments is how all of the subsequent postings create conversations. When you write a comment in response to someone's network update, every person who made a comment before you will receive an e-mail or other form of notification with the contents of your comment. In addition, when other people comment after you, you will receive all subsequent comments via e-mail or other form of notification. Also, just as with Facebook, some of your connections will ask you questions within your comments, and it is important to answer the questions or the conversation dies. In addition, as more people write comments, momentum builds and more people jump into the conversation.

In addition to writing comments in response someone's network update, or the subsequent comments from others, LinkedIn gives you the ability to "Like" a network update. This is the easiest way to contribute to a conversation without having to write anything creative. All you need to do is simply click the "Like" link to the immediate left of the "Comment" link. Once you click the "Like" link, it transforms into an "Unlike" link. In my opinion, this is not as useful as it is on Facebook, where your name is recorded as someone who "Liked" the post.

InMail Messages

Just as Facebook has its inbox messaging system, LinkedIn offers what it calls InMail®. In my experience, I have found it to be a bit cumbersome to use because to whom you can send a message is dependent on the degree of connection you have with a person. For example, with a first-degree connection, you are directly connected to someone. When one of your connection invitations is accepted, you become a first-degree connection with that person. You also have first-degree connections with anyone who belongs to the same LinkedIn groups as you do. LinkedIn allows you to send InMail messages to your first connections for free as part of your basic account.

LinkedIn only permits you to send InMail messages to second- and third-degree connections if you are using an upgraded (paid) account. Conversely, on Facebook, you can send a private inbox message to anyone on Facebook, whether you are friends with that person or not.

With that said, the process of sending a LinkedIn InMail message is simple. The first step is to open your list of connections by rolling your mouse over the "Contacts" tab in LinkedIn's top navigation. Then, scroll down the list, and click on the name of the person to whom you would like to send a message.

Once you click on the person's name, LinkedIn will provide you with the basic profile details to the right of your connections list. Once you click on the person's name to whom you want to send an InMail message, LinkedIn will display that person's basic details to the right of your screen. Within the basic details, LinkedIn provides several links — one of which is a "Send message" link. When I click on the "Send message" link, LinkedIn provides me with the InMail message window, which looks similar to the screen shot shown in Figure 4.23.

Figure 4.23 LinkedIn's InMail form

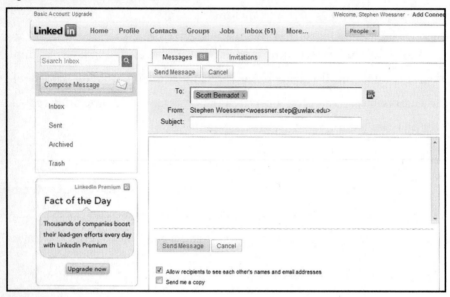

LinkedIn Corporation © 2010

LinkedIn pre-populated the "To:" field with Scott's name, which leaves me with completing the subject and message I want to send to Scott. When I finish composing the message, I simply need to click the blue "Send Message" button. The box "Allow recipients to see each other's names and e-mail addresses" is checked by default by LinkedIn. I do not see any reason to uncheck this box so I have always left it checked.

LinkedIn Groups: Joining and Creating

Joining a LinkedIn group is a good way to find a collection of like-minded people who share a common interest. Membership is free so I encourage you to take full advantage of this feature.

LinkedIn groups essentially works like message boards, where members can post questions in the hopes that fellow group members can offer advice or recommendations. Other people use groups to share updates about specific topics. LinkedIn groups act like a subcommunity within LinkedIn, and I highly recommend you look for topics that might interest you and begin participating. Or, if you do not find a topic that interests you, I recommend creating your own LinkedIn group. But, you do need to be somewhat selective in the groups you join because LinkedIn limits you to membership in 50 groups.

You can easily find and begin searching LinkedIn's list of groups by rolling your mouse over the "Groups" tab in the top navigation. When you do, a drop-down list will appear, which will look similar to the screen shot shown in Figure 4.24.

Figure 4.24 Finding LinkedIn groups

LinkedIn Corporation © 2010

Because you are just beginning the process, you will want to click on the "Groups You May Like" or "Groups Directory" links. If you click on the "Groups You May Like" link, LinkedIn will compare the content of your profile with the profile of its various groups and make recommendations to you. If you click the "Groups Directory," LinkedIn will provide you with a screen containing its "Featured Groups."

LinkedIn also provides you with several search options on the left side of the screen. You can choose to search for featured groups by category. The categories are All categories, Alumni group, Corporate group, Conference group, Networking group, Nonprofit group, Professional group, or Other. LinkedIn also allows you to specify the language used within the group.

However, if neither the "Groups You May Like" or "Groups Directory" links provide you with an interesting option, you might want to consider clicking the gold "Create a Group" button. When you click the link, you will receive a screen similar to Figure 4.25.

From this screen, you can create your own LinkedIn group and make the focus of the topic as specific and targeted as you like in order to attract the right connections. You will want to carefully consider the access questions that LinkedIn asks at the bottom of the screen. Would you like to grant "Open Access" so any LinkedIn member can join the group without prior approval from you, or would you prefer to establish a "Request to Join" policy? In my opinion, both options can work well, but there are trade-offs to consider. If you require a request to join, you may attract fewer members. But, the members you do attract may be more targeted for the conversation you are trying to create versus attracting members who are simply looking to join a bunch of groups to meet new people.

Figure 4.25 Creating your own LinkedIn group

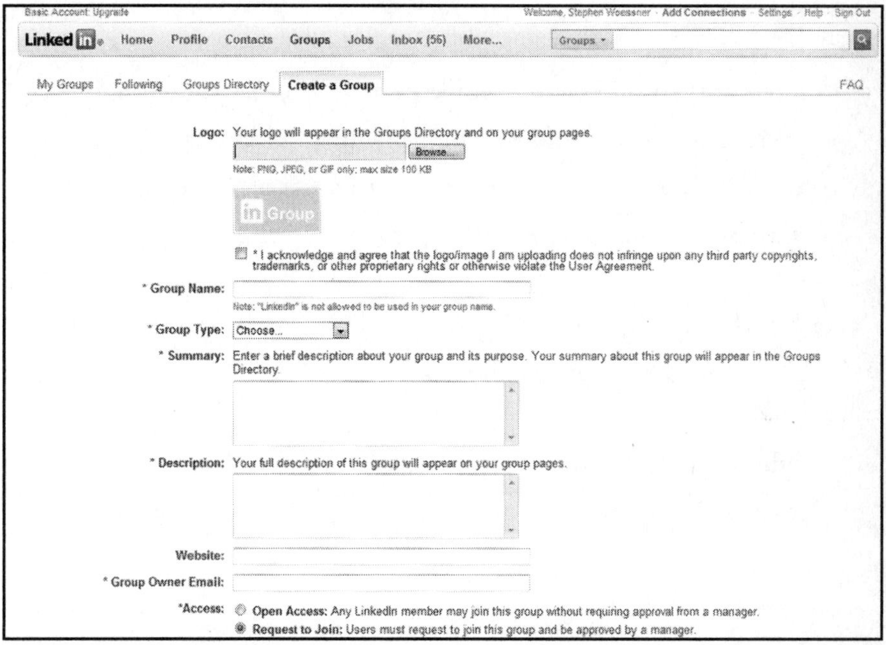

LinkedIn Corporation © 2010

Viral Social Networking Checklist: Part 4

❏ Sign up for your free LinkedIn account at **www.linkedin.com**.

❏ Search for people you already know who use LinkedIn by allowing the network to search your e-mail contacts file.

❏ Confirm your e-mail address by clicking on the link within the verification e-mail that LinkedIn sent to your e-mail inbox.

❏ Enter the e-mail addresses of colleagues and friends to whom you want LinkedIn to extend an invitation to join you on LinkedIn.

❏ Select a premium or basic (free) LinkedIn account.

❏ Complete your LinkedIn profile by adding a photo, entering current and past employment information, adding links to your website(s), linking the profile to your Twitter account, and writing your professional summary.

❏ Ask your clients and colleagues to endorse you by writing a recommendation you can post on your profile.

❏ Adjust your account and privacy settings to your desired comfort level.

❏ Write your first network update.

❏ Begin commenting on the network updates of your connections to get the conversation flowing.

❏ Send a couple of your connections an InMail message to become familiar with how the process works.

❏ Search for existing LinkedIn groups to join and request membership. Or, create your own LinkedIn group if you cannot find a suitable existing group.

❏ Proceed to Chapter 5: Building Your Online Community.

Building Your Online Community

Viral social networking steps covered in this chapter:

▸ **Step 5:** Announce your social networking participation to customers and prospects.

▸ **Step 6:** Expand your sphere of influence by learning how to add Facebook friends, Twitter followers, and LinkedIn connections to your online community.

I wrote the initial four chapters of this book with the goals of providing you with:

▸ A solid foundation for why viral social networking should be considered as an important promotional tool for your business

▸ How viral social networking works conceptually

▸ Overviews of the top three social networks — Facebook, Twitter, and LinkedIn

▸ How to get started using each of the three networks

I designed each of the foundational chapters to give you the necessary tools to efficiently and effectively implement the remaining 11 steps of the viral social networking process. In the chapters that follow, the true fun begins. Through your implementation of the checklists found in Chapters 5 though 10, you will begin to experience increased online sales and website traffic.

Chapter 5 will begin your journey toward increasing your online sales by providing you with specific detail regarding Steps 5 and 6 in the process. In Step 5, you will learn how to announce to your customers and prospects that you are now actively participating in Facebook, Twitter, and LinkedIn — and not with just a simple statement like, "Hey, come find me now on Facebook." You will learn how to maximize your efficiency and effectiveness by applying five different promotional tactics that will help you make your announcement as impactful as possible with your customers and prospects.

In Step 6, I will demonstrate in specific detail how you can increase your sphere of influence by growing the size of your online brand community. With Step 6, you will branch out and attract people to you and what you represent. By doing so, you will begin receiving Facebook friend requests, notifications that other users want to follow you on Twitter, and invitations to join other user's LinkedIn networks.

Steps 5 and 6 are also exciting because your efforts will be quickly measurable. You will likely experience tangible results, such as more friends, more connections, more followers, or even an increase in online sales shortly following the implementation of these two steps. In addition, because measuring results is so critical to your overall success with viral social networking, this book also goes into detail about how to collect and analyze the right data so you never have to guess how you are doing. *See Chapter 9 for more information.*

Step 5: Announce Your Social Networking Participation to Customers and Prospects

Your customer and prospect lists represent the "low hanging fruit" in your sales cycle. You might have heard this term before. It is a popular expression in the world of sales strategy used to describe the customers and/or prospects who are the easiest for you to convert into sales. These people are the easiest to convert into sales because they are already familiar with your products and services or perhaps know you personally. Because of this familiarity, it should require less time and money to generate new sales from this group versus attempting to convince someone who is not currently aware of you or your value proposition.

It makes sense to begin the viral social networking process by giving you all of the tools and resources you need to persuade as many of your existing customers and current prospects to join your online brand community. This will maximize your efficiency and effectiveness by helping you quickly develop a foundation of Facebook friends, Twitter followers, and LinkedIn connections.

Step 5 includes the following five tactics, each of which will be explained in specific detail:

1. Feature your social networking addresses within your promotional collateral materials, such as brochures, sell sheets, letterhead, business cards, or any other materials you print or produce to help promote and run your business.
2. Include clickable links to your social networks within your e-mail signature.
3. Place clickable logos within your website design template.

4. E-mail your customers and prospects.

5. Launch a promotion with incentives.

Featuring social networking addresses within promotional materials

Do you remember when it seemed a little strange or unusual to add your e-mail and website addresses to your business cards or other promotional collateral materials you used to promote your business? I remember thinking to myself back in the early '90s, "Who in the world is really going to type in this silly address and visit our website?" Now, it seems the opposite is true; it seems strange to see a business's promotional material without this information. Having a functional and interesting business website and using e-mail proficiently have become fundamental to doing business today.

It is now time to prominently feature the direct addresses — or links — to your Facebook, Twitter, and LinkedIn pages within all your promotional collateral materials, including business cards, brochures, letterhead, stationery, folders, sell sheets, invoices, television commercials, print ads, and billboards. Absolutely everything you print and use to promote your business should include your social networking addresses. Prominently featuring these addresses — or their logos — within your promotional collateral materials should become as commonplace as including your phone number(s).

The direct addresses — or links — to your social network pages will look somewhat similar to the following examples:

▸ Facebook: **www.facebook.com/people/Stephen-Woessner/ 614556212**

‣ Twitter: **www.twitter.com/stephenwoessner**

‣ LinkedIn: **www.linkedin.com/in/stephenwoessner**

You can find your specific social networking addresses by going to your various profile pages and copying the URL from the Web browser.

But, including the direct addresses as shown before is just one option. And after reading the next section, you will hopefully agree that it is not the best option.

If you type in the direct Facebook address to my profile (**www.facebook.com/people/Stephen-Woessner/614556212**), and you were not already one of my Facebook friends, you would receive the Facebook welcome screen that includes the public version of my profile, which includes my photo and a random list of eight of my friends. The sole purpose of this welcome page is to help visitors validate that you successfully found the actual "Stephen Woessner" you wanted to find.

Facebook displays the person's profile photo on the left of the screen, photos of several of that person's friends in the middle of the screen, and listings of the movies, music, and books that the person likes along the bottom of the screen. However, beyond this information, the welcome page does not share any details that might motivate someone to send the person a friend request. This is a missed marketing opportunity in my opinion.

As an alternative, I recommend that you consider printing each of the social network logos along with an address that takes visitors to a specific content page within your website instead of a welcome page like the one shown in Figure 5.1. The following is an example of how this might look on the back of a brochure:

Join us on FACEBOOK

Stop by. Say hello, and be in the know.

www.badaxetoolworks.com/bad-axe-tool-works-facebook.html

Facebook is a trademark of Facebook, Inc.

If someone were to type this address into their Web browser, he or she would be taken to a Web content page similar to the one shown in Figure 5.1 instead of the generic Facebook welcome screen reviewed earlier. A company called Bad Axe Tools Works™ (**www.badaxetoolworks.com**) owns this orientation content page. The company specializes in producing high-end saws for the discriminating woodworker. The saws are designed and fashioned by Mark Harrell whose goal is to produce saws that are consistent with the spirit of the Bad Axe river region in southwest Wisconsin.

Figure 5.1 Bad Axe content page

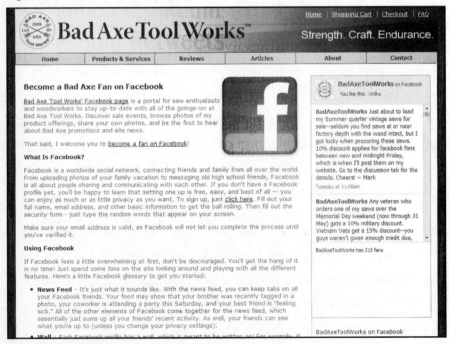

The content of the page is excellent because it provides visitors with brief and succinct information about the company's participation on Facebook. The page also serves as the first step in introducing the Bad Axe Tool Works website visitor to Facebook, including some reasons why a person should "Like" the Bad Axe Facebook page and some basic instructions on how to use Facebook.

It would be a mistake to assume that because Facebook has more than 500 million members worldwide, everyone has heard of it or understands what Facebook is all about. The same goes for the Twitter and LinkedIn social networks. Providing visitors with orientation content pages similar to the Bad Axe Tool Works example serves as a professional and helpful intermediary between your website and your social networking pages.

The large Facebook logo featured within the Bad Axe orientation content page is a direct link to the company's Facebook page. Once clicked, a person can officially "Like" the Bad Axe page or send a friend request if the page is a personal Facebook account like mine.

Please be sure to read all of the acceptable use guidelines regarding each of the social networks logos and/or trademarks before you begin adding the Facebook, Twitter, and LinkedIn logos to your website or promotional collateral materials. The logos are free to use; however, each network has different policies about the usage of their logos. None of the policies are overly complex, but the details do need to be reviewed. You can find all of the information on using the Facebook, Twitter, and LinkedIn logos at the following websites:

▸ Facebook Brand Permissions Center
   (**www.facebook.com/brandpermissions/**)

- ▸ Guidelines for Use of the Twitter Trademark
  (**http://help.twitter.com/entries/77641**)

- ▸ LinkedIn Logo Use and Download
  (**www.linkedin.com/static?key=branding**)

I would like to add a final comment before moving on to the second promotional tactic. Some business owners reading this book might want to incorporate their social networking addresses into their promotional materials as soon as possible, but I recommend that you prepare to make the updates in a more "phased approach" to be realistic from a financial management perspective. Please do not throw away perfectly good brochures, business cards, and so on and then print all new materials so you can add your social networking addresses. In fact, I think that would be a poor use of cash.

Instead, I recommend you begin adding your social addresses when materials are reprinted, a new television commercial is filmed, or your billboard layout is redesigned. The phased approach will still ensure a coordinated and integrated multimedia promotional campaign over time, and it will also help you preserve cash flow by avoiding significant production expenses occurring all within a short time.

Including clickable links within your e-mail signature

I try to make it a habit of not generalizing too much, but I suspect we all write and respond to plenty of e-mails every single day as part of our busy day-to-day lives. Each "signature" within the e-mail messages you send has the potential to serve as a mini-billboard or advertisement for your business — just like in the viral marketing Hotmail example highlighted in Chapter 1. The key is to ensure that the information you include within your e-mail signature does not cross the line of being too promotional.

The following is an example of a typical e-mail signature:

John Smith
Owner
Company XYZ
P: 555.555.5555
F: 555.555.5555
C: 555.555.5555
www.companyxyz.com

The typical e-mail signature is functional and succinct. It provides recipients of the e-mail message with all of the basic contact information they might need to connect with the sender. John Smith's e-mail address was not included within the signature because the recipient of the message can simply click the "Reply" button to obtain John's address or copy it from the header of John's e-mail message.

As an alternative, the following is an e-mail signature that I recommend you consider using as part of your strategy to announce your social networking participation. This e-mail signature will help you maximize your efficiency and effectiveness. It informs your e-mail recipients that you are actively participating in social networking and provides the links they need to find your various social networking pages.

The following is an example of a viral social networking e-mail signature:

John Smith
Owner
Company XYZ
P: 555.555.5555
F: 555.555.5555

C: 555.555.5555

www.companyxyz.com

Facebook: www.yourcompanyurl.com/facebook

Twitter: www.yourcompanyurl.com/twitter

LinkedIn: www.yourcompanyurl.com/linkedin

The only difference between the typical e-mail signature and the viral social networking signature is that the latter includes links to the social networking orientation content pages within your website. If you choose to create these orientation content pages, they should be similar to the Bad Axe Tool Works example highlighted in Figure 5.2.

I recommend including the addresses to your orientation content page within your e-mail signature versus including the direct links to the generic welcome pages on Facebook, Twitter, and LinkedIn. I make this recommendation because I believe it is always in your best interest to bring customers and prospects to your website in the most efficient manner possible. Bringing customers and prospects to your website as their first stop, versus your generic welcome pages on Facebook, Twitter, and LinkedIn, provides you with the opportunity to close online sales with this group of people more quickly. The majority of the people who receive your e-mails on a daily basis are likely your customers and prospects. And remember, these people represent the "low hanging fruit" in your sales cycle. By directing your customers and prospects to your website as their first destination, you are one step closer to increasing online sales, and increasing online sales is the primary goal of this 15-step process.

You would miss out on some immediate website traffic if you were to direct your customers and prospects to your generic welcome pages of Facebook, Twitter, and LinkedIn via your e-mail signature. If you sent prospects directly to the social networking sites, you would have to rely on those customers or prospects finding and visiting your website at some point in the future. A percentage of your customers and prospects will indeed visit your website, especially when you implement the remaining steps of this viral social networking process, but it is always in your best interest to bring them to your website as soon as possible because there is no advantage to you in waiting.

Placing clickable Facebook, Twitter, and LinkedIn logos within your website design template

The first two tactics in Step 5 provided you with recommendations regarding how to promote your social networking participation to primarily your current customers and prospects. I use the word "primarily" because typically the people who receive your print collateral materials via mail or trade show or your e-mails are likely somewhat familiar with you or are already doing business with you. Otherwise, they would not be included on your mailing list or corresponding with you via e-mail.

Now, it is time to announce your social networking participation to a group of people who may be completely unfamiliar with you or the products and services provided by your business. These people likely found your website by searching related keywords in a search engine.

This tactic also relies on the social networking orientation content pages that were highlighted in Figure 5.2. Now would be a good time to invest a few hours to create the three content pages because they will be used on a number of different occasions throughout the viral social networking process.

This section will assume that you already have social network orientation content pages on your website. The next thing to do is to download the Facebook, Twitter, and LinkedIn logos that are acceptable for use on a website. Sometimes, the acceptable use of the logos for a website is different than the acceptable use of the logos within print collateral. Please double check the acceptable use guidelines via the links that were provided earlier in Step 5.

Once downloaded, I recommend placing all three of the logos into your website template or cascading style sheet so the logos can be seen on every single content page throughout your website, similar to what is shown in Figure 5.2. *For more on cascading style sheets, see the CSS entry in the glossary.* You should see a "Follow Us" heading on the right side of the content page in the figure. You should also see the Facebook, Twitter, and LinkedIn logos under the header. These logos were added as part of the website's design template and appear on every content page within the website.

Figure 5.2 Add a "follow us" section to your website

If your website was created by a professional designer or developer, I recommend saving yourself the time and hassle of trying to figure this out on your own. In my experience, unless someone is familiar with editing website templates, it tends to be much more efficient and effective to simply provide the designer or developer with the logos and direct them where the logos should be placed within the site template.

When clicked by a website visitor, each of the logos should take the person to your respective social networking orientation content pages. The orientation content pages will provide you with an excellent opportunity to motivate the person to become one of your Facebook friends, Twitter followers, and/or LinkedIn connections. Remember, the addresses of your social networking orientation pages should be something similar to the following:

- Facebook: www.yourcompanyurl.com/facebook
- Twitter: www.yourcompanyurl.com/twitter
- LinkedIn: www.yourcompanyurl.com/linkedin

Sending e-mail campaigns to your customers and prospects

You might have already noticed this, but the first three promotional tactics within Step 5 tend to be somewhat passive versus proactive in nature. I label the tactics as passive because when your customers or prospects see your social networking addresses featured within your promotional materials and e-mail signature and the Facebook, Twitter, and LinkedIn logos placed prominently within your site's design template, they are the ones who are obligated to take action. They need to proactively click on the link within your e-mail signature or type your social networking address into their Web browser. The responsibility rests solely with the customers or prospects. This is passive promotion.

With the fourth tactic, I will show you how to become more assertive by distributing e-mail campaigns directly to the inboxes of your customers and prospects. The e-mail campaigns will specifically promote your social networking participation, provide direct access to your social networking orientation content pages, and encourage the recipients to visit and join your online brand community. The e-mail campaigns are proactive promotion because you will deliver a targeted and focused communication.

Before covering the how-to process of sending an e-mail campaign to announce your social networking participation, I would like to give you some insight into the results that two companies experienced from using e-mail as part of their promotional strategy. The first company is Dessert Gallery and the second is Bad Axe Tool Works.

Dessert Gallery

Sara Brook and the Dessert Gallery crew have been serving up sweet treats in Houston, Texas since 1995. The company's website (**www.dessertgallery.com**), shown in Figure 5.3, touts how the company puts smiles on people's faces at any of its convenient locations. As described on its website, the company believes that its stores are "a place where friendship is a delicate combination of admiration, trust, empathy, two forks, and one dessert." The Dessert Gallery is a place where "rich, chocolaty daydreams are served up, wonderful and warm-spirited, with a side of old-fashioned hospitality and relaxation." This seems to be the perfect recipe — pardon the pun — for social networking.

Figure 5.3 Dessert Gallery's home page

Copyright © 2010 Dessert Gallery. All rights reserved.

Successfully promoting Dessert Gallery via e-mail marketing and social networking is exactly what Sara and her team have done. I first learned about

Dessert Gallery when I read an article titled, "One Café Chain's Facebook Experiment" in the March 2010 issue of *The Harvard Business Review*. The article did an excellent job of reporting the results of a Facebook experiment conducted by Utpal Dholakia, an associate professor of marketing at Rice University, and Emily Durham, the founder and president of Restaurant Connections. The goal of their study was to determine if business pages on Facebook actually influence the consumer behavior of the customers and prospects. The following are the highlights of the article:

‣ The study began with the researchers distributing a Dessert Gallery survey via an e-mail campaign to 13,270 customers from the company's mailing list.

‣ The goal of the initial survey was to gather store evaluations and data on shopping behavior.

‣ A total of 689 people responded to the initial survey.

‣ The researchers then launched the Dessert Gallery Facebook page and invited everyone on the company's mailing list to become a fan or "Like" the page via another e-mail campaign.

‣ As part of the study, Dessert Gallery updated its Facebook page several times per week with product pictures, news about contests and promotions, links to favorable reviews, and introductions to employees.

‣ After 90 days, the researchers distributed a second survey via an e-mail campaign sent to the same sample that received the initial survey.

‣ The second survey received 1,067 responses, which was an increase of 378 people, or 54.8 percent.

▸ The researchers then analyzed the data collected from the two surveys and compared the results.

The results? The researchers concluded that Dessert Gallery's Facebook presence changed customer behavior. The customers who had responded to both surveys and had "Liked" the Dessert Gallery Facebook page were determined to be the company's best customers.

For example, even though these customers spent about the same amount of money per visit to Dessert Gallery, they increased their number of store visits per month after becoming Facebook fans by visiting the store 20 percent more often than non-fans. These customers generated more positive word-of-mouth advertising than non-fans. The customers also gave the store the highest share of their overall dining-out dollars. These customers were also the most likely to recommend Dessert Gallery to friends.

As a word of caution, only 283 or 2.1 percent of Dessert Gallery's mailing list customers actually became fans during the three-month study. The article also reported that in an analysis of 50 Zagat®-rated (**www.zagat.com**) Houston restaurants, their Facebook pages averaged just 340 fans despite their thousands of customers. However, as I write this chapter of the book, the Dessert Gallery Facebook page has increased its number of people who "Like" it from 283 to 817, an increase of 188 percent.

I thought the Dessert Gallery example was relevant for this chapter because the company accomplished much more than validating the potential of social networking as an effective business promotional tool. From my perspective, their cutting-edge research study provided additional insights into the positive effects of word-of-mouth communications and its role within the viral social networking process detailed within this book. In addition, I believe Dessert Gallery demonstrated the effectiveness of e-mail campaigns for distributing promotional announcements, such as launching the Dessert Gallery Facebook page and collecting research data via online surveys.

Bad Axe Tool Works

One of the tremendous benefits of using e-mail campaigns to announce your social networking participation is you might also generate immediate online sales as part of the strategy. This makes e-mail marketing an efficient and effective promotional tactic for your viral social networking strategy because increasing online sales is the ultimate goal no matter which path your customers or prospects use to get to your website to complete an order for your products or services.

Bad Axe Tool Works was successful in accomplishing both goals: It increased the number of people who "Liked" its Facebook page by introducing its social networking participation to its customers and prospects, and it increased online sales by introducing the company's two newest products: 12-inch and 14-ich models of its high-end woodworking saws.

The e-mail campaign that Mark Harrell, owner of Bad Axe Tool Works, created and distributed contained more content than the typical campaign. But, one of the strategic advantages that Harrell has skillfully developed is the strength of the personal relationships with his customers and prospects. From my perspective, his customers and prospects share a real passion for his products and a mutual respect for woodworking, which he shares with them. Consequently, his audience is very interested in the content he distributes because it is timely, valuable, and relevant to the recipients.

I will use Harrell's first e-mail campaign that he distributed as an example. The e-mail essentially contained two parts, which are shown in Figures 5.4 and 5.5 respectively.

Figure 5.4 Bad Axe Tool Works campaign, part 1

Bad Axe 12" Carcase ($195) and 14" Sash ($210) Saws Start Shipping April 15th

12" Carcase Saw Deposit

14" Sash Saw Deposit

Two Payments: By clicking one or both of the PayPal buttons above, you're making a $100 deposit to lock your place in the queue. After I complete the build I will invoice you for the balance due plus shipping. Shipping begins April 15th. *Wait times determined by deposit first-come, first serve.*

Carcase, Sash, & Facebook too--and that's our story! *(new developments from Bad Axe Tool Works)*

Hi Everyone!

I'd like to extend my deepest appreciation for supporting TechnoPrimitives and Bad Axe Tool Works over the past year, and want to fill you in on what's happening right now, because "Times," as Robert Zimmerman used to point out, "are a' changin'!"

My 12" Carcase & 14" Sash saws start shipping in mid-April.

Look for optional walnut handles, and steel split-nut fasteners when customizing the appointments of your saw. Here's how you lock in a spot in the queue for the first production run, until I get the new product pages loaded on my website:

Step #1: Just select one of the PayPal deposit buttons at the left.

Step #2: After making a deposit, shoot me an email including the information listed below:

General:

- Subject Line: I want to buy a Bad Axe 12" Carcase or 14" Sash Saw
- Your shipping address and contact information up front in the message.

Appointments: Specify the following:

- Cherry handle (standard) or walnut handle (add $10)
- Gunsmith-blued back (standard) or stainless back (add $10)
- Brass slotted nuts (standard)
- Stainless slotted nuts (add $10)
- Gunsmith-blued steel slotted nuts (add $12.50)
- Stainless split nuts (add $10)
- Gunsmith-blued steel split nuts (add $12.50)

Filing: Specify either your desired custom tooth configuration, or one of the standard configurations I list below:

©2010, TechnoPrimitives, LLC

Figure 5.5 Bad Axe Tool Works campaign, part 2

Bad Axe is Now on Facebook

Bad Axe now has its own Facebook page, and you'll find the link to it on my website at http://www.badaxetoolworks.com/bad -axe-tool-works-facebook.html.

Now I will freely confess to being a saw geek, and bear the classification with pride. You can be a saw geek too, and the discussion form on the Bad Axe Facebook page is already proving to be a great forum with which to ask questions and get them answered. Check out the topics have been developing over the past two months:

- How much is too much restoring of old saws?
- Optional Wood Species for Saw Handles
- What NOT to buy (in a vintage saw)
- eBay 'go-to' Saw guys
- How to buy an eBay saw: avoid the turkeys!
- Advantages of a longer dovetail saw
- Relaxed Rake: Where and Why
- Plate Thickness
- Japenese pull saws vs. Western saws—which do you prefer?
- What is size of back saw do you reach for the most in YOUR workshop?
- The Perfect nest of Saws

Part 1 of the e-mail — Figure 5.4 — focused on introducing the new saws. In addition to including photos of the new products and describing several of the product features, Harrell masterfully explained how the recipient of the e-mail can secure his or her saw by making a deposit via PayPal. This is outstanding, and I will explain why in just a moment.

Part 2 of the e-mail — Figure 5.5 — focused on introducing the company's participation on Facebook. There are two aspects of the Bad Axe Facebook introduction with which Harrell did really well. First, the e-mail directed people to visit the company's social networking orientation page on the Bad Axe website versus the generic welcome page on Facebook. Again, this brings customers and prospects directly to the Bad Axe website and provides the company with an opportunity to shorten its timeline for increasing online sales. Second, Harrell used the Bad Axe Facebook page as a tool for sharing how-to content that his Facebook fans really like. So, instead of just promoting the Facebook logo and a link to the website's orientation content page, he decided to include a sample of the content that Facebook fans are able to access via the company's Facebook page. This gave customers and prospects a preview of the valuable content they could access once they "Liked" the Bad Axe Facebook page.

The results? Bad Axe experienced two measurable results from its e-mail campaign: an increase in online sales and an increase in the number of people who "Liked" the company's Facebook page. More specifically, Bad Axe closed 30 new orders for its high-end saws within approximately 72 hours of sending the e-mail campaign. The majority of these orders were from existing customers who wanted the new 12-inch or 14-inch saws. However, the e-mail campaign was also successful in closing orders for the company's initial product line with prospects who had been on the Bad Axe mailing list but for whatever reason had not yet placed an order until receiving the e-mail campaign.

In addition to increasing online sales, the number of Facebook fans for Bad Axe increased from 140 to 217 at the time of this writing. This represents a 55 percent increase — not bad for one e-mail campaign.

Bottom line? Both Dessert Gallery and Bad Axe Tool Works successfully expanded their online brand communities by promoting their social networking participation via e-mail marketing campaigns. In addition, both companies increased sales through the combination of expanding the number of Facebook fans and introducing new products to their customers.

E-mail distribution systems

Using a sophisticated, yet inexpensive, e-mail distribution service like Constant Contact® (**www.constantcontact.com**) levels the playing field for small business owners and provides a high return on investment from both a time and financial perspective. Constant Contact is the system that Mark Harrell from Bad Axe Tool Works uses to create his e-mail campaigns. I have personally used Constant Contact to create and distribute hundreds of e-mail campaigns over the past five years and think it is a terrific value. I still wonder how the company can provide the level of service and reporting detail it does for the nominal monthly cost the company charges. Plus, Constant Contact serves hundreds of thousands of clients so you will not be a beta test client. The company delivers a proven platform for promoting your products and service via e-mail marketing in a spam-free environment.

One of the benefits that Constant Contact provides a business owner is the level of detailed reporting. For example, you can review the specific number of people who open your e-mail campaigns, what day and time each person opened the individual campaigns, which pieces of content each person clicked on — this is measured in click-through-rate, or CTR — and whether your e-mail was forwarded by one of your recipients to someone not on your e-mail list. Moreover, this is just a quick recap of all that is possible.

Constant Contact has also started investing resources toward integrating its e-mail distribution service with the power of viral social networking. This integration is another reason why I decided to include a somewhat in-depth overview of Constant Contact within this chapter.

This integration is accomplished primarily through Constant Contact's feature of adding logos and links to your online brand community — Facebook, Twitter, and LinkedIn — within your e-mail campaigns. Figure 5.6 is a good example of this new feature. When creating the e-mail campaign, you have control over the destination or link that you assign to each of the social networking logos. For example, for the Facebook logo, you could still link the e-mail campaign over to your Facebook orientation content page on your website instead of directing your e-mail recipients to your generic Facebook welcome page.

Figure 5.6 Adding logo links to your e-mail campaigns

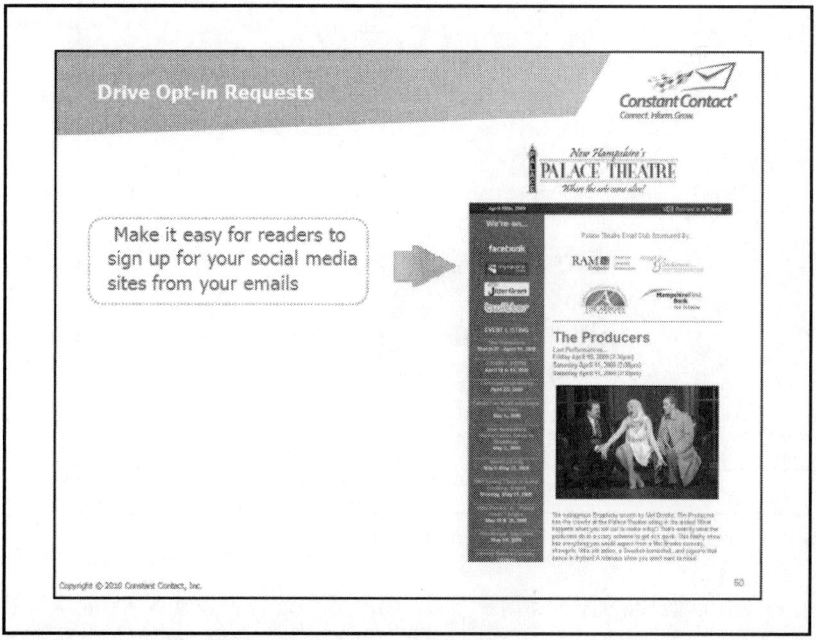

You can also use your e-mail campaign to promote any new content within your online brand community. For example, suppose you just uploaded a new video to YouTube and posted a link to the video on Facebook, Twitter, and LinkedIn, as shown in Figure 5.7. Instead of linking to the video directly from your e-mail campaign, you could include the link to where the recipients could find the video within your Facebook page so you pull people into your Facebook page instead of pushing them toward YouTube. Yes, you want them to see the YouTube video, but if you bring them to Facebook to find the YouTube video, your customers and prospects can browse through the other interesting content you have invested time and energy in building. This increases your return on investment.

Figure 5.7 Including social media in your e-mail marketing

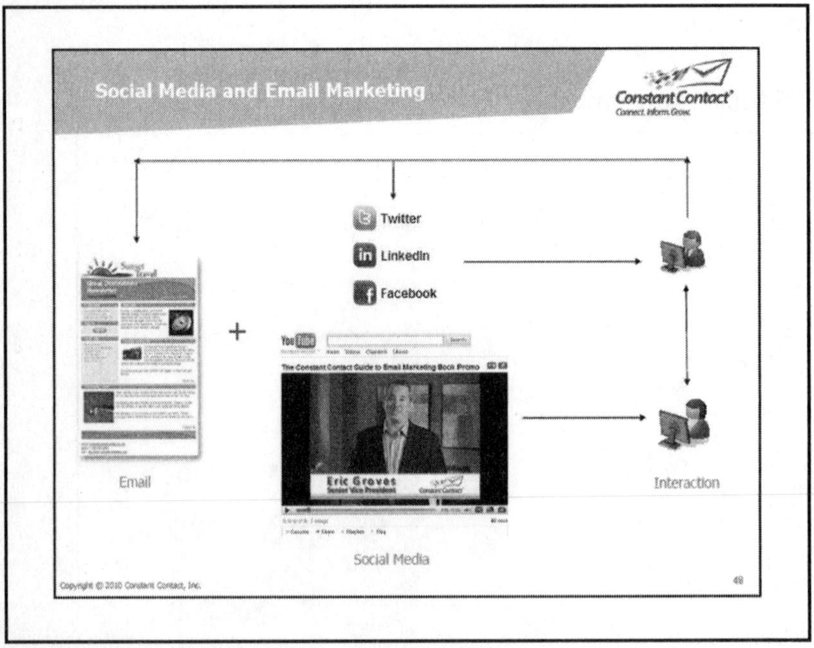

Constant Contact recently acquired a startup company called NutshellMail® (**http://nutshellmail.com**) to further entrench itself in the expanding world of viral social networking. You can learn more about the free service at its website. I have been experimenting with NutshellMail for several weeks, and to say that I am impressed would be a significant understatement. It compiles the activity taking place within your online brand community and delivers it right to your e-mail inbox in about ten batches a day. NutshellMail is an incredible tool that will help you maximize your efficiency and effectiveness. This is exactly why NutshellMail made my list of favorite viral social networking tools that I profile later in this book. *See Chapter 8 for more details.*

Within Constant Contact's website, you will find a number of informative and easy-to-follow tutorials inside the "Learning Center" tab. Each tutorial will help you get started with creating your first e-mail campaign. Constant Contact also provides hundreds of e-mail templates to choose from. All of the templates are customizable with your own content, photos, graphics, colors, and more. You do not need to know HTML or other forms of Web programming to efficiently and effectively use Constant Contact. Moreover, at the time of this writing, the company offered a free 60-day trial, which is an offer that is tough to beat.

I recommend the following if you would like additional how-to assistance beyond what the Constant Contact website offers:

▸ Call the Constant Contact toll-free customer support service team at 866-876-8464. I have called when I experienced problems with customizing a particular template I wanted to use. The company's team fixed the problem while I was on the phone with no hassles.

▸ I also highly recommend getting a copy of the book *The Constant Contact Guide to Email Marketing* by Eric Groves. Groves is the senior vice president of global market development at Constant Contact.

From my perspective, he did a great job writing a comprehensive guide that provides practical and tactical advice regarding the ins and outs of how to successfully use e-mail marketing in your business. You can find his book at Amazon.com, Barnes and Noble, and other book retailers.

Launching a promotion with incentives

The final tactic is to consider offering a promotional campaign with the goal of incentivizing more people to become your Facebook friend or your company's Facebook fan, follow you on Twitter, or connect with you via LinkedIn. Papa John's® is one measurable example of a company being successful with this tactic.

Papa John's experience using Facebook was reported in a March 9, 2009 story appearing in *BrandWeek Magazine*. *BrandWeek* described how Papa John's gave anyone who became a "fan" of its Facebook profile an online code worth a free pizza. This was a generous offer and seemed relatively easy to obtain. To help promote the incentive, Papa John's purchased an ad on Facebook and also sent an e-mail campaign to its customer database.

The results? According to Facebook, 131,000 people became fans of Papa John's within just a single day. Papa John's popularity within Facebook has continued to grow since the conclusion of the campaign. At the time of this writing, Papa John's Facebook fan base had grown to more than 1.3 million. At the time of the *BrandWeek* story, Papa John's was considered the second-fastest growing brand on Facebook. Unfortunately, the story did not include any data regarding Papa John's success in converting Facebook fans into buying customers or long-term customers, which should be the ultimate measure of success considering the cost of giving away more than 100,000 pizzas was significant.

I would be remiss if I did not offer a word of caution when implementing a promotional tactic such as this. One of the reasons that Papa John's was successful when it offered this incentive is because their brand name is well known and they could financially afford making such a generous offer in exchange for an increase in Facebook fanship. I would never recommend that you implement a promotional tactic that has the potential to be counterproductive to the goal of increasing your online sales. Consider the trade-offs and financial impact of any incentive you offer. With the power of viral social networking, you might receive a significantly higher response rate than you anticipate.

Step 6: Expand Your Sphere of Influence by Learning How to Add Members to Your Online Brand Community

Step 6 of the viral social networking process will deliver substantial value to your business because it was designed to help you accomplish four important objectives:

1. Increase your level of awareness within your local business community.

2. Enhance your expertise among your peers within your industry.

3. Expand your sphere of influence by increasing the size of your online brand community.

4. Strengthen relationships with existing customers.

You will be able to accomplish all four of these objectives by implementing the five tactics within Step 6. Ultimately, you will receive Facebook friend requests, notifications for people who are following you on Twitter, and invitations to join other's LinkedIn networks. Overall, your online brand community and sphere of influence will expand.

The five tactics within Step 6 are:

1. Remain active with Twitter.
2. Become a guest speaker within your community.
3. Get quoted in the media.
4. Write and share your expertise.
5. Get on the professional speaking circuit.

Remain active with Twitter

Later in this book, you will learn a specific process for distributing your Web-based content to your online brand community, which will of course include how to distribute content via Twitter. *See Chapter 7 for more information.* But, I would like to single out one aspect of that distribution process and address it here because it is directly related to your ability to attract more followers on Twitter. This involves how well you maintain your activity level within Twitter — meaning the number of Tweets you make a day, as well as how consistently you maintain that level of Tweeting.

While I am writing this chapter, there are currently 211 people following me on Twitter (**www.twitter.com/stephenwoessner**). Figure 5.8 is a screen shot of my Twitter page. This is a low number of Twitter followers, especially for someone who is supposed to be a social networking expert. Rest assured, there is a "method to my madness" as the expression goes.

Figure 5.8 My Twitter page

My number of Twitter followers is low because I am constantly testing and re-testing new theories that will hopefully lead to new online marketing strategies. What I have found through my extensive experimentation with Twitter is that the number of Tweets I send each day has a direct impact on the number of followers I attract. For example, during one of my experiments, I sent as many as eight Tweets in one day. This number of Tweets attracted 20 new followers. On the surface, 20 new followers in one day sounds like a decent result.

But, on that same day, five people quit following me by "unfollowing" me from their list. I made two observations based on the data regarding why this happened. First, the eight Tweets I sent provided substantial content for prospective followers to find during their Twitter searches, which led people to my Twitter page and subsequently increased my number of followers by 20 that day. But there are trade-offs to everything. My eight Tweets also annoyed five followers because some people really do not like what is called "hypertweeting." Paul McFedries, author of the excellent book *Twitter Tips, Tricks, and Tweets,* defines hypertweeting as posting an excessive number of Tweets.

From my perspective, writing as many as eight Tweets each day was not the answer. The results described earlier led me to begin adjusting my daily number of Tweets. Eventually, all of the testing I conducted showed me that two Tweets per day was ideal for producing the optimal level of website traffic and increases in online sales. Two Tweets per day also virtually eliminated the number of people who unfollowed me. This is the proper balance. Twitter will likely account for about 10 percent or more of your total website traffic if you follow this viral social networking process.

I will give you some additional insight while we are on the topic of Twitter research. From my previous experiments, I collected enough data on the power of Twitter for generating traffic when daily Tweet activity is optimal. So now, I am testing the reverse.

As I write this chapter, I am testing the decline or attrition of website traffic referred from a Twitter account when the person sends Tweets sporadically or seemingly random in frequency. I want to know, if I stop Tweeting, will my Twitter followers still represent approximately 10 percent of total website traffic as they did when I sent two Tweets per day? My initial theory was no, of course not. But, I would never have imagined what my initial data seems to be pointing toward.

For example, when Twitter represented 10 percent of total site traffic to my site, Twitter was also the No. 3 source of traffic. According to Google Analytics, the No. 1 source of traffic to my website was "direct" traffic. *See Chapter 9 for more information in Google Analytics.* You can get a head start by opening your free Google Analytics account at **www.google.com/analytics**. A site receives direct traffic when a visitor bookmarked a website during a previous visit and then uses the bookmark to return to the site. The return visit is logged as direct traffic. A site also receives direct traffic when a visitor types a site's address "directly" into his or her browser versus clicking on a link on search engine's search results page.

The No. 2 source was organic search traffic from Google. Again, these results were based on two Tweets per day. During my current experiment, I dropped my number of Tweets from two per day to once a week or even just two Tweets per month. The initial results? The amount of traffic coming from Twitter quickly dropped from being the No. 3 source to No. 12. The No. 12 position represented just 1 percent of total site traffic.

I realize that some might argue that it is counterproductive to allow the site traffic from Twitter to drop precipitously as I am in the current experiment. Moreover, the experiment has likely reduced online sales because the portion of my online brand community that Twitter represents is not growing as it should because of the lack of Tweeting. However, I have always felt that it is important to invest my own time and money to observe and understand the relationship that exists within the data so you can confidently implement the recommendations. I will likely post the final results of my current Twitter experiment on my blog on my website.

Become a guest speaker within your local business community

I heard a funny statistic recently, and it went like this: "The No. 1 fear among people is the fear of public speaking, while the No. 3 fear is the fear of dying. Which means the typical person would rather be the one in the box at the funeral instead of the one giving the eulogy." Therefore, I understand if you bristle at my recommendation to offer your services as a guest speaker within your local business community if you are not already doing this as part of your overall promotional strategy.

Unfortunately, these types of guest speaking projects are normally done for free, but they can provide you with substantial value worth much more than nominal compensation. I have highlighted what I consider the four main benefits of guest speaking in case it is not something you are currently doing on a consistent basis, which I consider to be six to 12 times per year. Guest speaking will provide you with:

▸ An additional platform from which you can demonstrate your expertise

▸ An opportunity to reach a new segment of customers and prospects who might be completely unaware of you and/or your business

▸ The perfect venue to further enhance your professional credibility, especially if you speak at some well-known events or organizations

▸ An opportunity to distinguish yourself from your competition

You will quickly develop a reputation within your local business community as someone who has a great message to share as soon as you complete several speaking projects for your local chamber of commerce or other economic development-oriented groups. People take notice of a high-quality guest speaker, and quite frankly, good speakers who are willing to give of themselves to help out their local community are sometimes hard to find. Because of this, you will likely begin receiving requests once the people who schedule speakers in your community hear about your success and desire to help.

The following are seven basic steps I recommend you consider for getting the process started:

1. Identify three to four business-oriented topics in which you have experience and are in line with the products and services your business sells.

2. Prepare two or three presentations in varying lengths from 30 to 60 minutes. This gives you the flexibility to accommodate various time slots with each group.

3. Contact your local chamber of commerce and speak to its events coordinator and offer your topics for consideration.

4. Reach out to your local Small Business Development Center (SBDC) and offer your services as a guest speaker or potentially an instructor for one of their education programs. You can find the SBDC nearest you at its website (**www.asbdc-us.org**). It is common for SBDC to be searching for new speakers and/or ad hoc instructors to teach the classes it offers.

5. Schedule the events and deliver excellent presentations.

6. Ask a friend or colleague to shoot photos or video of you in front of the group as you deliver your presentation, as well as candid shots of you talking with participants before and after the event. Promotional assets like these photos will become very valuable to you later in this book. *See Chapter 7.*

7. Lastly, make sure the last page of your handouts or presentation includes all of your contact information, as well as the addresses to the social networking orientation content pages on your website.

If you do not already own a copy of *The New York Times* best-selling *The 4-Hour Workweek* by Timothy Ferriss, I highly recommend you get one. Ferriss does an excellent job of providing readers with a five-step action plan that he calls "The Expert Builder: How to Become a Top Expert in 4-weeks." You can find the plan on pages 159 and 160. The plan is easy-to-follow and simple to implement and becoming a guest speaker is step three in the process.

Each speaking engagement adds what Ferriss describes as "credibility indicators," and I could not agree more. I have witnessed firsthand the power of credibility indicators in how people perceive another person. Several weeks ago, I was interviewed by *Inc. Magazine*. I was the same person before and after the interview, but once people knew about the interview, their perception of me shifted a bit and I somehow had more credibility. I know, it may sound silly, but it happens. So, all I can recommend is that you benefit from the phenomenon, too.

My final advice on this tactic is to be patient and relax. Start small. Complete several projects. Build some confidence. Branch out, and introduce yourself to larger organizations and perhaps some statewide events if or when you feel comfortable to do so. Before long, you will begin receiving Facebook friend requests, seeing an increase in your number of Twitter followers, and receiving LinkedIn network invitations from attendees who listened to you speak.

Get quoted in the media

Offering your services as a guest speaker will put you out in front of customers and prospects who might, at the time of hearing your message, be completely unaware of you until they see and hear you speak at an event they attend. In addition, it is common for the hosting organization of the event to prepare and distribute a press release regarding the event agenda, including who will speak, the date, and the times, to attract attention from the media.

When this happens, you will likely be presented with interview opportunities with the reporters from the various media in your area who are interested in covering the major themes of the event. Exposure on your nightly news, on a local radio show, or in your newspaper's business section is highly valuable because this type of exposure provides much more credibility than any advertising you could ever produce. Make sure you take advantage of any and all of these opportunities that come your way as a result of your work as a guest speaking.

I recommend that you begin proactively seeking interview opportunities with journalists who cover stories in your industry once you feel comfortable sharing your expertise with reporters. I make this recommendation for two important reasons. First, being featured in publications or other media that cover your industry will expose you to a larger audience of customers and prospects. Instead of perhaps 50,000 subscribers for a local newspaper, you and your message could reach 500,000 subscribers. And second, the stories written will connect well with your areas of expertise so you will be positioned as an industry expert.

But, the process for contacting all of the journalists covering your industry will be time consuming. You would also have no idea when you make the calls whether the journalist is even working on a story that is relevant for your expertise. Thankfully, there is a better way. In my opinion, ProfNet® is the best service at effectively connecting subject matter experts — you — with journalists who are working on stories they are writing now. ProfNet (**www.profnet.com**) is a division of PRNewswire.

More than 100 journalists use ProfNet every single day. You will receive "opportunities" or leads e-mailed directly to your inbox approximately ten times per day. Each opportunity summarizes the focus of the story, what the reporter needs, the deadline, and how you can contact the journalist if you have the expertise the story needs. When I joined ProfNet, my strategy was only to respond to online marketing-oriented opportunities that were exact matches to my experience. I did not want to waste a journalist's or my own time if I did not think the opportunity was perfect for my experience. Consequently, I only responded to three opportunities during my first week of using ProfNet. Yes, only three opportunities — but I was successful in getting three interviews with each of the journalists. Even one interview would have been significantly more than the number of interviews I could have generated on my own. Plus, my total time commitment for responding to the journalists and providing them with the interviews was less than one hour. Getting one interview per month within a well-known publication is a good benchmark to pursue.

Visit the *E-Commerce Times* website (**http://tinyurl.com/2ar8azy**) for an example of an interview that came my way via ProfNet.

An annual membership to ProfNet costs approximately $1,000 depending on the type of business you operate. I rationalize this cost by estimating that five to ten stories in targeted industry publications will provide a suitable return on investment.

In addition to the interview opportunities you find via ProfNet, some journalist might also find and contact you directly as your reputation as a trusted industry expert grows. For example, last fall I was contacted by the *Milwaukee Journal Sentinel* completely out of the blue for my opinion regarding the success a Wisconsin business owner was having with search engine optimization. You can find the story online on the newspaper's website at **www.jsonline.com/business/65911392.html**. I did not do anything special to attract this opportunity. You can have the same success by making yourself available and willing to share your expertise.

Getting interviewed is critically important to your viral social networking strategy because a percentage of the people who read the stories containing your quote(s) will send you Facebook friend requests, begin following you on Twitter, or send you invitations to join their LinkedIn network. This expands your online brand community by adding people potentially from across the country or even globally. But, perhaps more importantly, these people already believe you have something good to share with them because they were likely impressed with the quotes from you, or they never would have initiated the connection.

Share your expertise by writing

A certain level of credibility is bestowed upon the person who authored an article, white paper, or book. If you happen to enjoy writing, you can leverage this credibility to your advantage in several important ways:

▸ The articles and papers you write will expose you and your message to a new audience of customers and prospects, similar to when a journalist interviews you as an expert for a story.

▸ Your published work will make you more attractive to organizations as you seek out future speaking engagements.

▸ Your published work will also make you more attractive to journalists for future stories because you have established a tangible record of your expertise.

▸ The content you write will provide additional traffic to your website as the articles and papers are indexed by search engines.

▸ All the content you write will become a valuable asset you can share with your online brand community. *See Chapter 7 for information you need to follow to share the content so it provides you with the maximum benefit.*

A percentage of the readers of your published work will search for you on Google, Yahoo!, Bing, or another search engine. The search results might direct them to your website or the generic welcome pages to your

Facebook, Twitter, or LinkedIn profiles. Regardless of the path the readers choose, you will begin receiving Facebook friend requests, additional Twitter followers, and invitations to join the LinkedIn networks of people who might not have known you otherwise. All of this helps you expand your online brand community.

The following steps can help you get started:

▸ Contact your local newspaper, speak with the business editor, and offer to serve as a guest columnist or some other form of contributor.

▸ Contact the local business magazines in your community, and offer to write a consistent column on relevant topics to their readers.

▸ Write articles, and submit them to relevant trade journals for consideration.

▸ Begin a blog on your website, and post your latest content. *See Chapter 6 for information on how to leverage the assets of blog content into additional website traffic.*

And lastly, be sure to provide journalists with a byline for yourself that reads something like, "John Smith is the president of Company XYZ. Find him on Facebook, Twitter, and LinkedIn." This helps inform readers of your participation in social networking.

Get on the professional speaking circuit

I recommend that you consider doing some professional speaking if you find the guest speaking, media interviews, and writing about your areas of expertise to be enjoyable. You do not need to stop running your business or put your life on hold to pursue professional speaking opportunities. However, it is not for everyone. Making a name for yourself and building a high-quality reputation as a professional speaker is a serious time commitment. The speaking business is competitive with plenty of great speakers, some of whom likely already address your areas of expertise.

With that glowing endorsement, why in the world would anyone want to make the effort? First, professional speaking can make you well known to a large number of people at the same time. Again, the goal is to expand your online brand community. Presenting yourself and your message to a large audience at one time provides you with an efficient and effective way to reach plenty of people in a short time.

Second, professional speaking can be financially rewarding. Several of my friends who are professional speakers typically command fees for keynote speaking in the neighborhood of $20,000 to $50,000 for each speech. Lou Holtz, a family friend, has set his speaking fee at $40,000. Holtz is one of the most successful coaches in college football history. His 1989 team at the University of Notre Dame won the national championship. I have had the privilege of watching him deliver one of his motivational speeches, and he is worth every penny of his speaking fee.

There are as many as 120 speaking bureaus in the United States that you can approach for representation. I am represented by multiple bureaus, one is a company called Leading Authorities, Inc. in Washington, D.C. Leading Authorities has been in business for 19 years, and in my opinion, they are world-class. Leading Authorities is also an award-winning production house.

Leading Authorities has been excellent at supporting my professional speaking ambitions. They developed a high-quality bio page on their website (**www.leadingauthorities.com/Speaker/Stephen-Woessner.aspx**) shown in Figure 5.9. The staff at Leading Authorities also connected me with various other speakers who have acted as mentors to me and shared their valuable experience regarding the best strategies for getting started in the speaking business.

Figure 5.9 My bio on Leading Authorities' site

Perhaps more important than the fees you might earn on each speaking engagement is the efficiency and effectiveness you will have added to your schedule. Professional speaking could provide you with the ability to generate significant revenue in a short time — such as the duration of each event. This revenue might afford you the luxury of investing more time toward strategizing new products or services that could open up new channels for your business, generate new opportunities for media interviews, or give you new ideas for articles to write. All of these things could lead to more speaking engagements and an online brand community that continues to expand.

Viral Social Networking Checklist: Part 5

❏ Feature your social networking addresses within your promotional collateral materials by using the addresses of your website's orientation content pages.

❏ Begin using a viral social networking version of an e-mail signature for all of your e-mail correspondence with customers and prospects.

❏ Place Facebook, Twitter, and LinkedIn logos within your website design template after reading all acceptable use guidelines.

❏ E-mail your customers and prospects via Constant Contact or another e-mail distribution system, and announce your social networking participation.

❏ Launch a promotional campaign with the goal of incentivizing more people to become your Facebook friend or fan, follow you on Twitter, or connect with you via LinkedIn.

❏ Remain active with Twitter by consistently writing two Tweets per day.

❏ Become a guest speaker by contacting your local chamber of commerce, Small Business Development Center office, or another organization to offer your services at their events. Deliver excellent presentations, and capture video and photos of yourself before, during, and after each event.

❏ Make the process of being quoted in the media as efficient and effective as possible by signing up for ProfNet (**www.profnet.com**).

❏ Write and share your expertise by contacting the local media and offering your services as a guest columnist, writing articles for relevant trade journals, and posting content to a blog on your website.

❏ Contact speakers bureaus like Leading Authorities (**www.leadingauthorities.com**) to begin the process of getting on the professional speaking circuit.

❏ Proceed to Chapter 6: Give Your Community Members What They Want — Great Content.

Give Your Community Members What They Want – Great Content

Viral social networking steps covered in this chapter:

▸ **Step 7:** Write effective and persuasive social networking posts that share aspects of your life and business with your online community.

▸ **Step 8:** Create compelling content your online community wants that will increase your website traffic.

▸ **Step 9:** Increase conversion rates by as much as 780 percent by blending product or service-related links into your Web-based content.

My goal with Step 5 of this process was to provide you with a practical and tactical blueprint that would help you announce your social networking participation to all of your customers and prospects. Step 6 demonstrated how you could expand your sphere of influence and attract people to you and what you represent. My hope is that you have begun to experiment and apply what you learned during Chapter 5 and have already witnessed some initial results.

Chapter 6 is exciting because you will learn how to provide the members of your growing brand community with the content they want. Equally important, this chapter prepares you to master Steps 10 through 13 of the process, which focus on the distribution of your content. However, we must first create the content before any results can be enjoyed.

Steps 7, 8, and 9 in this chapter will provide you with an exact recipe for creating the new, interesting, and persuasive content that the members of your brand community expect. In Step 7, you will learn how to write Facebook status updates, Twitter Tweets, and LinkedIn network updates that are effective at communicating the message you want to share with your brand community.

In Step 8, you will learn how to efficiently and effectively invest your time toward developing blog posts, website content pages, Facebook photo albums, podcasts, and YouTube videos. Each type of content fulfills a specific role and engages the members of your brand community in a different way. The content you create is a key ingredient to creating additional conversation within your community, attracting additional members into your community so it continues to expand, and establishing the foundation you need in order for your community to begin generating commerce. In Step 9, you will learn how to incorporate links within your product- or service-related Web-based content with the goal of increasing your online conversion rate by as much as 780 percent.

In short, Chapter 6 continues the journey you began with Steps 5 and 6 toward increasing online sales.

Step 7: Write Effective and Persuasive Social Networking Posts that Share Aspects of Your Life and Business with Your Online Community

I would like to address a typical concern with writing social networking posts before explaining the elements of what makes a particular post effective and persuasive. It has been my experience that many business owners and managers who are evaluating whether to get involved with social networking believe that they will run out of important or relevant things to share with their community members. Some people have gone as far as to say, "there is nothing particularly interesting about my life, so why would anyone care to read about it." Rest assured, I shared this same concern when I began using Facebook, Twitter, and LinkedIn.

I thought, "Who in the world is going to care about what I did today or the people I met? I had some meetings across campus, it was a sunny day, I worked on some typical projects this week, and I wrapped up the next chapter in my book. Who will honestly care about any of that?" To my surprise, I found that my Facebook friends, Twitter followers, and LinkedIn connections not only cared, but they also offered encouraging comments regarding what I was sharing on a daily basis. Ultimately, this led me to discover that the more I shared what sometimes felt like the minutia of my life for others to see, the more comments I received.

It is also important to realize that it is likely the majority of the members within your brand community will never post a comment regarding your status updates, Tweets, or network updates. People enjoy the voyeuristic aspects of Facebook, Twitter, and LinkedIn. Your members will appreciate being able to peer into aspects of your life, see what is going on, perhaps make a comment or two in order to stay in touch, and then move on. However, even if the majority of your members do not post comments, this does not mean they did not read the information you shared.

For example, I frequently bump into my Facebook friends, Twitter followers, or LinkedIn connections around town at the grocery store, a restaurant, the mall, or while I am traveling. When I do, the person will typically start the conversation by saying something like, "Wow, it sounds like you are traveling all over the place and things with the book are going well. Are you ever home?" What I find interesting is that each time this happens, it is obvious the person has read, and perhaps more importantly remembered, my social networking updates even though he or she did not post a comment.

Therefore, keep in mind that the members of your community will scan and read your social networking posts just like newspaper headlines. And, just because they did not post a reply comment, your members are still reading and watching because they are interested in what you have to say.

Recommended topics

I hope I have successfully created a convincing argument that your members will be interested in the social networking updates you choose to share. I thought it might be helpful to share some recommendations regarding topics you might consider as you get started down the path of posting.

You will notice that the topics are divided into two categories of context: life/professional related and product/service related. A life/professional-related post means that the context of what you write revolves around you and not the products or services your company offers. The context of what you write will focus specifically on what happens in your life on a day-to-day basis from a personal and professional perspective, such as your achievements, your failures, projects on the horizon, insights into your family life, your travels, and other events. Rest assured, even the events you consider to be trivial could be perceived as very relevant to some of the members in your community. All of the details about your life that you choose to share creates conversation with your members, builds stronger relationships within your community, and establishes the foundation you need for commerce to take place. Some examples of life/professional-related topics might be:

- Attending a conference as a guest speaker
- Family outings, parties, vacations, or other travels
- Time with friends
- Birthday parties and holidays
- Moving
- Being contacted by media for an interview
- Blog post about your latest article to be published online
- Community events or nonprofit causes you support
- Your outlook for the week
- The trials and tribulations you experienced that day or week
- Brief description about some of the most important projects you are currently working on and what they involve
- Details of any interesting meetings you had that week

A product/service-related post means that the context of what you write revolves around the products or services your company offers. The context of what you write will focus specifically on attributes of the product, specifications, customer trials and satisfaction reports, warranty information, or trade shows the company will attend.

All of the intimate — non-proprietary — details you choose to share with customers and prospects creates conversation, increasing the company's credibility, and makes it possible for commerce to happen. Your product/service-related posts will also include embedded links to Web-based content that could facilitate the sale of your products or services. This will be discussed at length within Step 10 of the process. Some examples of product/service-related topics might be:

▸ Awards your product or service recently received

▸ Announcements of new product specifications

▸ Announcements of special offers, such as financing, pricing, or other terms

▸ Extension of product warranty duration

▸ Customer testimonials posted on your website

▸ Sales representatives or dealers added in certain territories

▸ Acquisition of a new division or company

▸ Product becomes available in a new geographic territory

▸ Addition of new employees

▸ Expansion or broadening of product and/or service offering(s)

▸ Company's products or services featured within trade journal(s)

▸ Attending a trade show along with an open invitation to visit your booth

▸ Details of product reliability tests and/or research findings

▸ Product or service-related blog posts

I recommend developing your own list of topics in each category that you anticipate being informative for the members of your community, as well as interesting for you to write about. It is all right if your initial list contains just a few topics or becomes a very long list. It does not matter at this point, as long as you begin getting your ideas down on paper because the list will be a helpful tool in keeping your social networking strategy focused in the future.

Elements of an effective or persuasive post

Have you ever been to a party when "that person" comes up to you and before you can even say hello, he or she begins bragging about what he or she did that week, how much money he or she made last year, the type of car he or she drives, or where he or she lives? After a couple of sentences with a person like this, my attention shifts, and I begin wondering how I can get myself out of the conversation as politely as possible.

It has been my experience that most people do not respond favorably to this type of boastful, self-centered communication style. Most people do not enjoy these conversations at parties, and your community members will not enjoy reading your social networking posts if you write them in this manner either. The result will be that your members tune out your message and eventually leave your community. Obviously, this is counterproductive to the goals you are working hard to accomplish.

Being honest and opening up your life in a truthful and humble way is the best way to develop long-lasting personal relationships, whether on Facebook or with your neighbors living next door to you. Given that, I believe there are four key elements to writing effective and persuasive social networking posts, which are:

1. Be humble. Do not brag.

2. Be honest and genuine.

3. Be factual and concise.

4. Embed a link to more information when relevant.

Your posts in either the life/professional or the product/service context are excellent opportunities to demonstrate your expertise. However, you must communicate your message in a humble, honest, and concise manner, or you will turn people off. Never extend or stretch what it is you can do. Never boast. Never brag. Never be dramatic. No one likes an arrogant blowhard who constantly toots his or her own horn.

Remember, some of your customers and prospects are in part reading your posts to help them determine whether aspects of your experience could benefit them and their business in some manner. If your capabilities are shrouded within arrogant and annoying statements, your entire message will be lost.

I will now dissect three of my previous social networking posts in order to illustrate the four key elements mentioned earlier. Two of the posts are life/professional related and one is product/service related.

Life/professional-related example

Earlier this summer, I received one of the biggest surprises of my professional career when a journalist with *Inc. Magazine* called to ask if I would help the magazine with a how-to search engine optimization guide for their July-August 2010 issue. I nearly fell over when I got the voice mail and heard the journalist's message. Needless to say, I quickly returned his call and scheduled the interview. Once the excitement of being interviewed had worn off a little bit and I could think a bit more clearly, I wrote a Facebook status update that read, "Got interviewed by *Inc. Magazine* for a story in their July-August issue about small business owners and search engine optimization." What I wrote adhered to three of the four key elements. I did not brag, I was honest and genuine, and the post was factual because I included the name of the magazine, the date of the upcoming issue, and the topic of the interview. The post was also concise because it only took 21 words to communicate the message I wanted to share. The results were that 11 people chose to "Like" the status update and 21 comments were written.

When this happens — and it will likely happen to you, too — it demonstrates engagement by your community members regarding the message you are sharing.

In the next example, I had been actively posting updates regarding numerous home improvement projects I had been doing for about six weeks in my previous house to get it ready to be sold. My wife and I had lived in the house for 15 years, and we had reluctantly decided it was time for more space. I shared the details of my drywall projects, installing a wood floor in my kitchen, family room, and hallway, wiring and lighting projects, and so forth. Throughout the process, I received what seemed to be an outpouring of positive and encouraging comments from community members. I did my best to give people access to what was going on at the house on a daily basis. Ultimately, we sold the house in five days.

So, when moving day finally came, I wrote a Facebook status update that read, "Tonight is Day 1 of moving. Loading the truck and beginning to say goodbye to the house we have lived in for 15 years. I love the new place, but I am so going to miss this house. Closing Friday and then finishing the move tomorrow night. Am happy and sad at the same time."

I think my community members were just as happy as I was to be closing out the chapter of home improvement projects and transitioning to life in the new house. What I wrote within this post again adhered to three of the four key elements. I did not brag about the new house, I was honest and genuine about the deep emotions I was feeling at the time of moving out of the old house, and the post was factual. I did not include a link to more information because it was not relevant regarding the context of the post. Overall, the post produced a conversation that contained 36 comments from my Facebook friends who wished me well with the move and life in the new house.

Product/service-related example

I recently wrote a product/service-related post on Facebook that read, "Got a request over the weekend to discuss Baidu versus Google in China as part of an international version of my SEO book. Now that would be super fun! And the book is now available in Japan."

What I wrote within the status update adhered to all four of the key elements. I did not brag about my SEO book now being sold in Japan. I was honest about the request I received regarding the writing of an international version of the book. I was genuine about the fun I would have working on this type of project. I was also concise by making the post in 36 words. And lastly, I included a link to the Amazon.com Japan website so members of my community could verify the accuracy of my post and visit Amazon if they felt it was necessary.

The results were that four of my Facebook friends "Liked" the status update and 20 comments were written within the ensuing conversation.

I would like to make one final comment regarding the link to Amazon. com Japan that I included within this post. I recommend that you only, on rare occasions, include links to content found on websites other than your own. The reason is that encouraging your community members to visit Amazon.com increases Amazon.com's website traffic but does very little, if any, to increase your own website traffic. But, including the link to Amazon. com enhanced the credibility of the product I am promoting, which in this example was my book.

What I should have done was write a blog post on my website regarding the new distribution in Japan, embed a link to the Amazon.com Japan site within my blog content, and finally embed the my blog link into the Facebook status update. Then, my community members who clicked on the link would have been taken to my blog as the first step versus directly to Amazon.com. In addition, within the blog post, I could have embedded an Amazon.com affiliate product link so if anyone had ordered the book, I would have received a commission from Amazon.com. I will discuss this in greater detail within Step 8.

In closing, I recommend that you resist the temptation to embed links to Web-based content in each of the social networking posts you write. If you include a link within each post, your efforts will become counterproductive because you turn your community into a selling free-for-all. Your members will not appreciate your attempts to overtly sell them your products or services. As a result, your community will shrink in size. Therefore, you need to share posts with a mixture of contexts. Step 10 of this viral social networking process will provide you with an easy-to-follow 6:1 ratio for your posts that will help you maintain the right balance.

Step 8: Create Compelling Content that Your Online Community wants that will Increase Your Website Traffic

Congratulations on completing the first seven steps of the viral social networking process. These critical steps provided a practical and tactical blueprint for building your online brand community and the process for writing effective and persuasive social networking posts that share your life, products, and services with your members.

Now, it is time to create the compelling content that your community members want. This content is different than the social networking posts discussed in Step 7. Step 8 is devoted to creating Web-based content that is compelling, intriguing, and influential with your online brand community members. Your compelling content will create interest among community members and help strengthen relationships. Ultimately, your compelling content will encourage and motivate your Facebook friends, Twitter followers, and LinkedIn connections to click on the links you share with them during Step 10 of this process.

Step 8 will provide you with the insights necessary so you can create compelling blog posts, website content pages, Facebook photo albums, podcasts, and videos through YouTube and Facebook. The majority of this content will reside within your business website — with the exception of Facebook photo albums. Consequently, your website traffic will increase when you distribute your content to community members during Step 10. Your website will receive an inflow of traffic from your Facebook friends, Twitter followers, and LinkedIn connections. It is likely that you will increase your website traffic by approximately 23 percent or more. Nine percent of this traffic will likely be your Facebook friends, nine percent will likely be from your Twitter followers, and the remaining five percent will be from your LinkedIn connections.

In my opinion, there are primarily seven critical elements or attributes of compelling content. Several of the elements can be blended together within one piece of content, but this does not have to be the case. The seven elements are as follows:

1. Follow word count best practices.

2. Follow keyword frequency best practices.

3. Make content visually interesting with photos and graphics.

4. Include headlines that capture interest.

5. Make a simple call-to-action.

6. Use photo albums to strengthen and deepen community member relationships.

7. Harness the power of video and/or audio.

I want to cover one more important point before getting into the details of Step 8. By incorporating these seven elements into the content for your community members, you will also accomplish another very important goal. Your content may also been seen as compelling by Google and other search engines. Moreover, these overlaps between viral social networking and search engine optimization are what make Step 8 one of my favorite steps within the entire social networking process.

For example, the word count within a website content page is a factor that Google uses when determining how to rank a content page within its search rankings. Google prefers content pages that are within a certain word count range. In addition, Google prefers website content pages that include a certain frequency of keyword usage. This helps Google quickly determine the focus of any content page.

Because of the importance of these two factors, I decided to pull in two excerpts from Chapter 6 of my first book, *The Small Business Owner's Handbook to Search Engine Optimization*. I included the excerpts because they are excellent examples for illustrating elements No. 1 and No. 2 of creating compelling content. These excerpts will give you insight into the ideal word count range for each of your content pages, as well as keyword frequency. The excerpts will provide you with the tools to incorporate SEO tactics into the content you worked hard to produce, which will further increase your results. Your overall online promotional efforts will be more efficient and effective.

Follow word count best practices

The following excerpt is from Chapter 6 of *The Small Business Owner's Handbook to Search Engine Optimization* and is titled "Remain within the word count range."

"Google prefers specific content pages toward a specific topic versus vague or general content. In addition, Google prefers that your specific content pages also fit within the parameter of 500 to 1,000 words per page. This is because if your content is too short, you will not have built up enough keyword frequency to highlight your optimization to Google. If your content is too long, Google will still index it, but if you exceed 1,000 words, the attention span of your human website visitors will likely wane, too. So, the 500 to 1,000 word guideline is exactly that…a guideline to help you balance Google's expectations and the needs of your website visitors.

I was recently asked by a participant during my Best Tactics for Online Marketing class at the university whether a product-specific page within an e-commerce website still needed 500 to 1,000 words. My answer was yes, although the realistic expectation would be to use the lower end of the range.

I would like to proactively address a potential misperception regarding word count. I realize the 500 to 1,000 words may sound high, but it is not. Let me give you another real-world example to help make this step in the SEO process more tangible.

Located on the University of Wisconsin La Crosse's website at **www.uwlax.edu/sbdc/CGBP-Series-2009.htm** is a content page I developed to promote our Certified Global Business Professional (CGBP) course on campus. This content page consists of 760 words. The way the content is displayed on the page gives the visual impression that it might be longer than it is. But more importantly, it provides Google with the amount of text it considers to be ideal: 500 to 1,000 words. In addition, the content does not discuss the overall international business education programs offered on our campus. The content page focuses specifically on the CGBP designation, which incidentally satisfies Step 9 in the SEO process."

I realize that not everyone enjoys writing and that sometimes it can be very challenging to write a description of the products and services you offer in a unique and different way. Try this simple exercise if you find yourself in the situation where you need to boost your word count in order to get within the 500 to 1,000 range. Try imagining if your very best prospect were to call you this morning. You answered the phone, and the client told you he or she needed a solution to a problem. As he or she described the problem, you saw an immediate fit with the products or services you could offer. But, the client also told you he or she had to make a quick decision and did not have time to review and analyze a bunch of different suppliers. This one call was your shot to close the sale. What message would you share with the client over the phone about your product or service that was unique, different, and compelling? Would you share recent customer testimonials? Would you talk about warranty or pricing guarantees, dependability, or time-tested performance? I bet the passion in your voice for what it is that you do would come through loud and clear on the other end of the phone. And, I suspect your message would be fall somewhere within the 500 to 1,000 word count goal. Get them down on paper, and you are well on your way to creating compelling content!

Follow keyword frequency best practices

The following excerpt is from Chapter 6 of *The Small Business Owner's Handbook to Search Engine Optimization* and is titled "Manage keyword frequency and prominence."

"Keyword frequency is the number of times a given keyword or keyword phrase is repeated within the same page of content (not your entire website — just the particular page of content being analyzed). Step 11 will provide some guidelines to follow that will ensure that your frequency and prominence meet Google's expectations. I will continue to use the UW-La Crosse CGBP content page as an example. Within the 760 words of content on this page, I repeated the usage of the keyword "CGBP" a total of 32 times. This represents the keyword frequency for this content page.

While a keyword frequency of 32 repetitions seems like a huge number at first, from both a visitor's perspective and Google's, the keyword frequency of 32 is actually quite appropriate.

If you visit the content page, you will see that I did not sacrifice the readability of the content page by achieving such a high frequency.

You will see that I strategically sprinkled the keyword "CGBP" throughout the full 760 words of content — from the top of the page all the way to the bottom. You will find the CGBP keyword in virtually every paragraph throughout the content. The content page still reads nicely; it is not clunky, as are some supposedly "optimized" pages that you have likely read on other websites and considered using as a model.

Here is a usage guideline to following when focusing on building your keyword frequency within your content pages. You should strive to reach a keyword frequency of eight to 46. Therefore, your goal should be to use your two keywords a total of eight to 46 times throughout the content page, from top to bottom. Just to be clear, I am not recommending that you use each of the two keywords eight to 46 times for a total keyword usage of 16 to 92. A frequency of 92 would seem ridiculous to users, and Google will begin to become suspicious and potentially consider your content page for keyword stuffing or spamming.

So, if your content is closer to 500 words, then your keyword frequency would be closer to eight. If your content is closer to 1,000 words, then your keyword frequency would be closer to 46."

Make content visually interesting with photos and graphics

You may recall the Mt. Hood story that I included at the beginning of this book. I shared the story with several friends and colleagues nearly immediately after I finished writing it. Some of the comments I received back were inspiring and got me thinking that the story could become a good blog post and potentially help introduce the upcoming release of the book you are now reading.

But, my Mt. Hood story as it appeared in book format was simply text. No graphics. No photos or anything visually interesting. I knew my blog readers would cruise right by the story if I posted the content in its current form. I needed to spice it up by including a photo of Mt. Hood. Figure 6.1 is a screenshot from my blog. You can find the Mt. Hood blog post at **http://seotrainingproducts.com/blog-life/climbing-mt-hood**.

Figure 6.1 Photos or graphics within content

Granted, finding a royalty-free photo and including it within a blog post is not an earth-shattering development, but compelling content does not have to scream at the reader in order to command attention. Creating visually interesting content can be as simple as including a photo or graphic that is relevant to the theme of the page. In this example, a single photo of Mt. Hood did the trick.

Including photos or graphics into your website content pages to make them visually interesting has an additional benefit beyond what is seen on the page itself. Step 10 of the social networking process will show you how to share or distribute your content to your community members via Facebook, Twitter, and LinkedIn. When doing so, Facebook quickly scans the content page being shared with the goal of finding a photo or graphic that it can include within your status update to make it more visually interesting.

Facebook realizes that photos and graphics make the status updates that people share more compelling so make sure to include these elements within your website content. Facebook will likely collect all of the photos and graphics from the content page and display as a series of thumbnails next to your post. When you are finished writing your post, you can select one of the thumbnails to become part of your post. Facebook will display the thumbnail adjacent and to the left of whatever you wrote.

Remember, your Facebook status updates appear in the news feeds of your community members. If you include photos within your updates, they will visually stand out from all the other posts within someone's news feed. The photo you include within your website content page could be the difference between someone clicking on the link to read the rest of the story or bypassing your post and clicking on someone else's.

Include headlines that capture interest

It has been my experience that website visitors tend to scan online content versus reading the content of a page word for word. The scanning process is very similar to the way most of us tend to read the newspaper. We scan for headlines looking for what might be an interesting story before we delve into reading each one.

You can take advantage of this scanning process by always including a headline at the top of each content page. The headlines will make your content more compelling and relevant to your visitors.

A compelling headline will stop a person who is scanning right in his or her tracks. The headline is likely concise and succinct. Because the headline essentially introduces the reader to the content found on the page, a compelling headline will always be in sync with the theme of the page.

Figure 6.2 is a screenshot of the content page found on my website at **http://seotrainingproducts.com/blog-life/google-website-ranking**. The page is an article that details the process of calculating the actual dollar value of a No. 1 ranking in Google for a specific keyword. Many people believe that having a No. 1 ranking in Google for a keyword is valuable. However, this is only partially true because a keyword only has financial value if people actively use the keyword every day to find content.

Assuming your keywords are actively used, this article provides a method for converting keyword usage and website traffic numbers into dollar value. Important stuff! I wrote the headline in the form of a question regarding dollar value because I suspected that most people who might read the information might have wondered the same question to themselves.

Figure 6.2 Website content page example

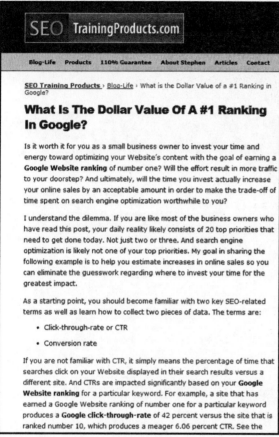

Here is one last piece of advice regarding writing compelling headlines. Do not put a lot of pressure on yourself in an attempt to write a masterpiece. Keep it simple. Remember — the purpose of a headline is to compel readers to view the rest of the content on the page. Do not spend hours languishing over whether your headline is compelling enough. Your Google Analytics statistics will show you if your community members are reading your content and how long they are staying on the page. Step 14 will teach you how to begin using Google Analytics to measure your results.

Make a simple call-to-action statement

Your content pages will further compel your website visitors if you include some form of call-to-action statement. Figure 6.3 is a screenshot of a product page that has blended the headline with the call-to-action statement.

Figure 6.3 Product page example

Call-to-action statements encourage a website visitor to take some form of action. In this example, the call-to-action is encouraging visitors to purchase the product featured within the content page.

However, many organizations use their websites to actively promote their products or services, but they do not conduct any e-commerce. These websites are for promotion only and not transactions. For example, I was recently teaching a class at a University of Wisconsin campus and one of the attendees was the marketing director for a physical therapy clinic. Obviously, the clinic's website was not going to begin selling physical therapy sessions online. But, the clinic could include a unique 800 number that can only be found online to easily track the number of monthly usages. Or, the website could contain a "Request More Information" e-mail, downloadable white papers from the therapists, or some type of questionnaire. All of these represent some form of call-to-action, and each time someone fills out a form or sends an e-mail, this represents an online conversion that can be measured to evaluate effectiveness.

Use photo albums to strengthen and deepen community member relationships

In my opinion, one of the most influential aspects of Facebook is the ability to create and share photo albums. The photo albums that you upload and share will help strengthen and deepen relationships with your community members. Your community members want to know more about you — otherwise they would have never accepted your friend request or sent you one in the first place. Your photo albums give them a glimpse into your life. Your photo albums, to some degree, give your community members the ability to experience the fun aspects of your life vicariously through your photos. Your community members will enjoy seeing your vacations, sporting events, birthday parties, and holidays and meeting all of your friends and family.

The comments you will receive on your photos will be touching, may be inspiring, and will demonstrate the connectedness you are developing with your community members. Do not feel like you only have to show the happy side of life. Remember, being genuine and real is an important part of participating in social networking. I encourage you to share the ups and downs of everyday life. Your community members want to get to know the real you so do not be afraid to share.

You can create your first Facebook photo album by clicking on the "Photos" tab at the top of your Facebook menu. The process of uploading and editing your photo albums is relatively intuitive once you get started.

Harness the power of video and/or audio

Podcasts and online videos can be compelling and can serve as excellent tactics for demonstrating your expertise to your community members. Both are compelling because they allow your community members to hear your voice, hear your expressions, and see your mannerisms. These are important because they give your community members additional insight into who you are, what you represent, and additional aspects of your life.

Have you ever watched one of the popularity reality TV shows, and as the weeks went on, did you began to identify with one or more of the players or characters? As shows like this progress, at-home viewers find ways to connect their own lives with the lives of those playing the game. That is one reason so many reality shows rely on viewer voting as part of the composite scores used to decide who stays in the competition and who goes home. At-home voting is an indication of the strength of the relationship that the characters or participants have with television viewers. And, the stronger the relationships are with viewers, the more votes are cast by viewers, which also influences ratings. At-home participation is an ingenious marketing strategy because of how it increases engagement with viewers.

You can use video and audio to increase engagement and the strength of your relationships with your community members in a similar, albeit less Hollywood, manner. Each time one of your community members downloads your latest podcast or watches your latest video on YouTube, you share your expertise and, in effect, strengthen your relationship with that person. The only caveat to this strategy is you need to be comfortable recording your voice, as well as being in front of a camera. If you are, then using podcasts and video could be ideal for you.

The main recommendation that I would like to make within Step 8 regarding podcasts and YouTube videos is that you make your website the access point to this content. For example, Figure 6.4 is a screenshot from the blog "Power to the Small Business" by Jay Ehret. Ehret is a marketing consultant in Texas who has developed a significant online following for his podcasts. *You can read more about him in the success stories featured in Chapter 10.* Whenever Ehret produces a new podcast, he always creates a landing page like the one shown in Figure 6.4 so that when he announces the podcasts availability via Facebook, Twitter, LinkedIn, or other promotional tool, he can be assured the prospective listeners will visit his website as their initial destination. The podcast in Figure 6.4 can be found on his website at **http://tinyurl.com/34cn77m.**

Figure 6.4 Podcast example

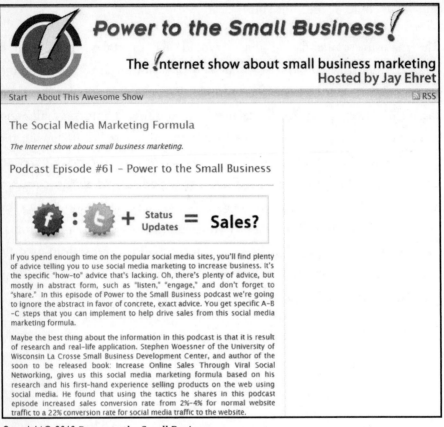

Power to the Small Business!

The Internet show about small business marketing
Hosted by Jay Ehret

Start   About This Awesome Show   RSS

The Social Media Marketing Formula

The Internet show about small business marketing.

Podcast Episode #61 – Power to the Small Business

f : G + Status Updates = **Sales?**

If you spend enough time on the popular social media sites, you'll find plenty of advice telling you to use social media marketing to increase business. It's the specific "how-to" advice that's lacking. Oh, there's plenty of advice, but mostly in abstract form, such as "listen," "engage," and don't forget to "share." In this episode of Power to the Small Business podcast we're going to ignore the abstract in favor of concrete, exact advice. You get specific A-B -C steps that you can implement to help drive sales from this social media marketing formula.

Maybe the best thing about the information in this podcast is that it is result of research and real-life application. Stephen Woessner of the University of Wisconsin La Crosse Small Business Development Center, and author of the soon to be released book: Increase Online Sales Through Viral Social Networking, gives us this social media marketing formula based on his research and his first-hand experience selling products on the web using social media. He found that using the tactics he shares in this podcast episode increased sales conversion rate from 2%-4% for normal website traffic to a 22% conversion rate for social media traffic to the website.

Copyright © 2010 Power to the Small Business.

I recommend that you use the same landing page example when you produce YouTube videos by embedding the video file into your website content. This will allow visitors to watch your YouTube video without ever having to leave your website content pages. Avoid promoting the direct website address to your YouTube channel because when your community members visit the YouTube address, you will not be able to measure the traffic, as it lies outside your domain. You can visit the home page of my website (**www.seotrainingproducts.com**) for an example.

Step 9: Increase Conversion Rates by Blending Product or Service-related Links into your Web-based Content

Suppose you invest your time and effort toward creating compelling blog posts, website content pages, and landing pages for your podcasts and your community members are increasingly becoming more engaged with you and your message. You are consistently receiving friend requests from all over the world. You are receiving e-mails from interested prospects who want to connect with you and learn more about what you do. In short, your sphere of influence is growing, as is the traffic to your website.

However, unless you have taken the time to blend in links to your products and services within the compelling content you produced, it is likely that your online sales have not reached their full potential. Rest assured that this is an easy fix with Step 9 of this viral social networking process. In addition, Step 9 also overlaps into search engine optimization, which is why I decided to pull in another excerpt from my book, *The Small Business Owner's Handbook to Search Engine Optimization*. Step 9 will help you increase your conversion rate by as much as 780 percent, and if you follow the advice in the excerpt, your search engine rankings will also increase.

The following excerpt is from Chapter 6 of *The Small Business Owner's Handbook to Search Engine Optimization* and is titled "Add anchor text links to content." The excerpt illustrates how to create the best links to benefit both your conversion rate and SEO.

"A link provides a valuable service to the visitors of your content pages by directing them to additional information that could be valuable to them. Plus, it helps you keep your content pages specific and links visitors to different topics — on equally specific content pages — within your website.

From an optimization perspective, Google likes pages with links because the links give them directions to additional content pages that they might not have had an opportunity to index otherwise. Therefore, Google pays a high degree of attention to the links that you include within your content pages. Consequently, you have an opportunity to get the most value out of your links by placing keywords within the link text. In fact, I recommend that the links within your content pages never look like the "click here for more details" format that you have likely seen many times and potentially still use within your website. Instead, I will show you how to create links that provide more value to your visitors, as well as to Google, by following two simple criteria:

1. Include your targeted keywords within the anchor text link at least once.

2. Use up to 15 words within the link to make it descriptive for the user and for Google versus the typical "click here" format."

Viral Social Networking Checklist: Part 6

❏ Develop your own list of life/professional-related and product/service-related topics using the recommended topics found earlier in this chapter as a starting point.

❏ Make your first life/professional-related post.

❏ Make your first product/service-related post.

❏ Create content pages that fall within the 500 to 1,000 word count range to make the information compelling and search engine friendly.

❏ Create content pages that include keyword frequency between eight and 46 repetitions to make the information compelling and search engine friendly.

❏ Make your content pages visually interesting by including photos and graphics.

❏ Help website visitors who tend to scan information by including headlines that capture interest.

❏ Include simple call-to-action statements within your content pages so visitors are motivated to take action.

❏ Upload one photo album to Facebook per month in order to strengthen and deepen relationships with your community members.

❏ Create a landing page for your podcasts and YouTube videos to reside, and then begin recording content that allows your community members to hear your voice, hear your expressions, and see your mannerisms.

❏ Blend links to your website's product- or service-related content pages within the compelling content you create as part of Step 8.

❏ Proceed to Chapter 7: Share Your Content to Your Community.

CHAPTER 7:

Share Your Content to Your Community

Viral social networking steps covered in this chapter:

▸ **Step 10:** Distribute content to your online community via status and network updates on Facebook, Twitter, and LinkedIn.

▸ **Step 11:** Follow a proven 6:1 ratio for the context of your social networking posts.

▸ **Step 12:** Build trust and genuine relationships with your online community members.

▸ **Step 13:** Manage your viral social networking strategy in just ten minutes a day.

The sole purpose of this chapter is to help you increase your online sales in the least amount of time possible. Steps 10 through 13 of the process will help you monetize all of the hard work you have invested up to this point.

You have built your online brand community and expanded your sphere of influence. You have invested time toward developing compelling website content. You have blended your product and service links into your content pages so website visitors can easily take action if they choose, and you have learned how to write effective and persuasive social networking posts.

It is now time to tell your community members where they can find your great content, while avoiding the temptation to turn your community into a selling free-for-all. You will also learn how you can further build trust with your community members through actively listening and responding. Lastly, you will learn how to manage the day-to-day activities of your social networking process in about ten minutes a day. Otherwise, if the time investment trade-off is too high, you will be too busy and the social networking process will never get done.

For example, I was recently invited to be a guest speaker at a university, and the topic was social networking and its benefits to nonprofit organizations. The group consisted of nonprofit executive directors and staff members who suspected that social networking could benefit their respective organizations. Some had even dabbled in social networking already, and some had board members who were active on Facebook, Twitter, and LinkedIn and were encouraging the nonprofits to get engaged with this new promotional tool. Because of the favorable demographics, and especially the income levels of Twitter and LinkedIn members, it seems reasonable to expect that social networking could provide participating nonprofits with access to more donors, volunteers, and other stakeholders.

However, because of my experience in serving on nonprofit boards, I also realize that most executive directors have been charged with seemingly impossible takes. Every day, they set out to do more with fewer resources — just like small business owners and today's busy manager. Therefore, when I introduced myself to the group I said, "Good morning, and I get it. You already have a full plate of projects. You have donors and volunteers to recruit, a board of directors to keep informed and engaged, concerns with staff that need fixed, and stakeholders your organization is dedicated to serving. So, I understand that if I fail to put all of the social networking benefits into a process that you can implement in ten minutes a day or less, it will never get done. That is the reality we all live in. Our schedules are maxed as we work hard to accomplish more with fewer resources."

When I finished my introduction to the group, I quickly scanned the room and looked into the eyes of the attendees. What I saw were some smiles. I saw that some of the stressful expressions had seemingly melted away. The message had captured their attention because they understood that what I was about to share could realistically get done within their already busy schedules.

If you are dealing with similar constraints — and I suspect you are — then you will *love* this chapter!

Step 10: Distribute Content to Your Online Community via Status and Network Updates on Facebook, Twitter, and LinkedIn

In Chapter 4, an example of a LinkedIn network update was provided where I had included a link to the Amazon.com Japan website. There was a missed opportunity within this example even though it made sense to share the Amazon.com Japan website link. The missed opportunity was that I could not measure the number of community members who visited the Amazon.com Japan website because I had not created a supporting content page on my website to act as the destination page. Instead, my community members were taken directly to Amazon.com. If time constraints prohibit you from developing a destination page on your website, then following the direct strategy like the Amazon.com Japan example is a suitable alternative, but it is not ideal.

But, there will also be instances when your status updates or posts are essentially that — just updates. You do not need to feel pressured to create a compelling content page on your website to support each of your social networking posts. There likely will be instances when new developments occur or some great news hits about your product or service, and you just wanted to get the word out to your community members as quick as possible. Make your own judgment calls, and balance the need for supporting content on your website. Although I have never formally measured this, I suspect community members would grow tired of seeing links within each and every one of your posts. So, take a break, mix it up, and do not feel pressured to create supporting website content all the time.

Figure 7.1 is a screenshot of a Twitter Tweet that distributes content while providing a supporting website content page as the initial destination for community members who clicked on the link. Although Twitter is featured within this example, the content within this Tweet was also used to make the posts on Facebook and LinkedIn.

Figure 7.1 Example of sharing a website content page via Twitter Tweet

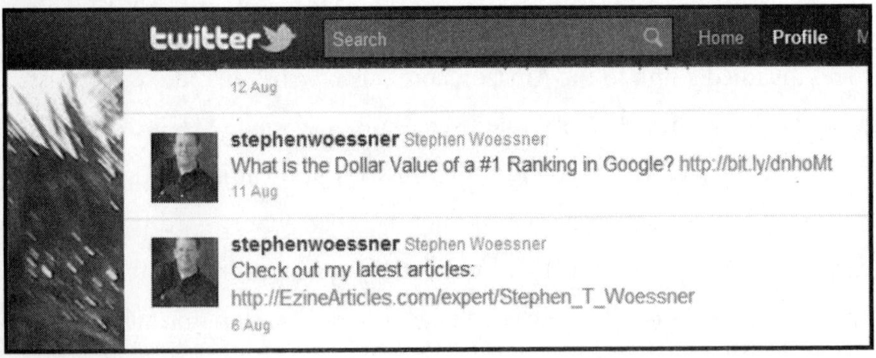
twitter
Search
Home
Profile
12 Aug
stephenwoessner Stephen Woessner
What is the Dollar Value of a #1 Ranking in Google? http://bit.ly/dnhoMt
11 Aug
stephenwoessner Stephen Woessner
Check out my latest articles:
http://EzineArticles.com/expert/Stephen_T_Woessner
6 Aug

© 2010 Twitter

The website traffic results generated by these posts were interesting. Figure 7.2 is a screen shot from my Google Analytics account that shows the increase in visits to my website as a result of the posts. The traffic from community members quantifiably increased weekly website traffic by 15 percent. Traffic from Facebook represented 29.7 percent of the total pageviews of the article that was shared. This was significantly more than Facebook's average of 9 percent. Surprisingly, Twitter only accounted for 2 percent of the total views, which was less than its average of 9 percent. LinkedIn did not generate any views, which was less than its average of 4 to 5 percent.

Figure 7.2: Specific pageviews for the supporting content page

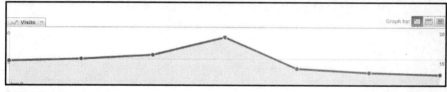

©2010 Google

In addition to people directly visiting the article, the amount of traffic hitting the overall website increased in a similar pattern as shown in Figure 7.3.

Figure 7.3: Overall website traffic

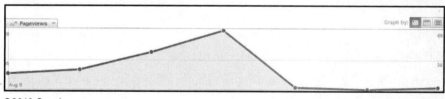

©2010 Google

The correlation in traffic pattern is likely because community members visit the specific content pages distributed via social networking posts, as well as take the time to visit the website's home page. Overall, you can assume that your website's home page will also receive an influx in traffic. In the case of this example, Facebook represented 25.3 percent of the total pageviews for the home page during this time. Step 15 of this process details how to install and use Google Analytics so you can analyze the same statistics for your website.

Now, it is time to briefly discuss the distribution process, which is functionally the same as the Amazon.com Japan example. The main difference between the two is that Step 10 has highlighted the benefits to writing social networking posts that direct your community members to supporting content pages on your website versus another site where you cannot measure the impact.

But, I will take this opportunity to highlight the similarities and one small difference between Facebook and LinkedIn in respect to posting links. Figure 7.4 shows the network update field on LinkedIn.

Figure 7.4: LinkedIn Network update field

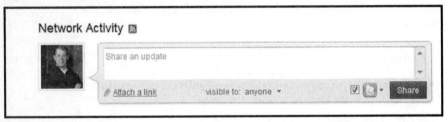

© 2010 LinkedIn Corporation

The update fields for both sites visually look very similar. The only difference, and it is a very slight one, is that within Facebook, you will need to click on the small "Link" icon directly under the Facebook text field in order to paste in the destination link to your supporting content pages. Within LinkedIn, you must click the "Attach a link" link as demonstrated during Chapter 4.

Ultimately, the process of distributing your content to your community members will only take minutes to complete. The majority of your time will be invested toward creating the supporting content pages on your website.

As an additional time saver, any of the posts made within your LinkedIn account can be automatically distributed to your Twitter followers and vice versa if you connect the two accounts during the setup process. *See Chapter 4, Step 4 of this process if you have some questions about how to connect the two accounts.*

Steps 13 and 14 will help you save even more time. The steps provide a daily checklist, as well as some advice on free tools, that will help you keep your daily time commitment to less than ten minutes a day — without sacrificing results.

Step 11: Follow a Proven 6:1 Ratio for the Context of Your Social Networking Posts

I mentioned earlier during Chapter 5 that at the beginning of my research, there were some days that I hypertweeted or wrote too many Facebook status updates or LinkedIn network updates. I made these mistakes because once I saw the data that showed increases in website traffic and online sales, it was tempting to send more and more sales-related messages to see what would have happened. The result would have been disastrous because I would have turned my community into a selling free-for all.

Thankfully, I never reached that point because some of my community members let me know that the number of messages I was sending, as well as the consistent context being product/service related, was in their opinion excessive. In addition, I experienced some people leaving my community by unfriending me on Facebook or unfollowing me on Twitter.

This was exactly the valuable feedback I needed in order to be able to modify my strategy and provide community members with the content they wanted in a non-intrusive manner. Here is the reality…writing too many social networking posts is the online equivalent of yelling or screaming at someone for attention. And rest assured, none of your community members want to be yelled at — either in person or online. You will receive their attention when they feel you have something worthy of interest or compelling to share and when you have built trust.

So, I went back to the drawing board and began experimenting with fewer posts per day. I also began experimenting with how often I should distribute a product/service-related post in relation to the number of life/professional-related posts I distributed. After 150 days of constant experimentation and adjustments, I discovered a very simple balance that I call the 6 to 1, or 6:1, ratio.

To produce the most website traffic and online sales, you should write six life/professional-related posts for each product/service-related post you write.

Following the ratio will provide your community members with the valuable and compelling content they want in a non-intrusive manner. The ratio will ensure that approximately 86 percent of your posts (100 percent ÷ 7 total posts = 14.28 percent x 6 life/professional-related posts = 85.70 percent) will be focused on increasing tie strength with your community members by sharing insight into your personal and professional lives. This makes the one product/service-related post that you make much more impactful, relevant, and welcome.

Step 12: Build Trust and Genuine Relationships with Your Online Community Members

In Chapter 1, I briefly explained the term "tie strength." Conceptually, tie strength measures the strength of relationships and the various factors within a particular relationship that connect any two people. Trust is one of those critical factors. Without trust, a relationship is fragile and does not blossom into all of the possibilities. And yes, you can build trust and genuinely strong relationships with your community members. But how?

You can build trust by listening and becoming actively engaged in the conversation. Facebook, Twitter, and LinkedIn provide you with an exceptional opportunity to listen to your friends, family, customers, prospects, and industry colleagues. When you are talking with someone close to you and you feel that person is hanging on your every word, it is likely you feel more connected with that person. You feel he or she is truly listening to what you have to say. You feel the person is interested in your thoughts, feelings, and what is going on in your life.

Obviously, a conversation via wall posts, comments, replies, inbox messages, chats, and direct messages are not replacements for spending time with someone offline and in person, but surprisingly, your social networking activity can, and will, help you develop genuine relationships among your community members. These relationships will progress to trust as long as you respect the boundaries and avoid the temptation of turning your community into a selling free-for-all.

I recommend that you make an effort to respond to the comments your community members post concerning your status updates. Trust will be built when your community members believe they can depend on you to listen and to respond to comments posted on your wall. Responding to comments is important so you do not create the inadvertent impression that comments are sent off into a black hole. If you do not respond in a timely manner, some of your community members might start to think to themselves , "What's the point… he/she won't ever get back to me so why bother," when considering commenting on your status. The result will likely be a lack of trust and weak relationships.

You can develop trust and tie strength with your community members by simply applying the following several guidelines:

▸ Write a comment within 24 hours to any wall postings your community members post on your Facebook wall.

▸ Scan your Facebook news feed and write comments regarding the status updates of community members or new photo albums that have been posted. Making five to ten postings a week is likely sufficient and not that time consuming.

▸ Check the "Events" section within the upper right corner of your Facebook news feed to see which of your friends is having a birthday. Then, write birthday wishes on the walls of those people to wish them well. This is a simple way to remind someone how special he or she is to you.

▸ Reply within 24 hours to any comments your community members post regarding your Facebook status updates or LinkedIn network updates.

▸ Reply within 24 hours to any Twitter direct messages you receive.

Lastly, by simply having a Facebook, Twitter, and/or LinkedIn account, you have already gone a long way toward expressing trust because your community members will be able to post public comments whenever they choose, assuming the privacy settings you selected allow this. This requires trust on your part. Unfortunately, some community members might abuse the trust you placed in them. Someone might decide to post questionable comments or content. The good news is that these are rare occurrences and easy to fix. You can delete the comments from your profile and choose to remove the friend if you feel it is appropriate to do so. Using the mobile applications from Facebook, Twitter, and LinkedIn make this even easier, allowing you to delete comments while you are on the move.

Step 13: Manage Your Viral Social Networking Strategy in just Ten Minutes a Day

You do not have to be on Facebook, Twitter, and LinkedIn all day in order to be successful with social networking. And, if you are like the majority of the small business owners and managers I know, you probably do not have the luxury of assigning someone within your organization the full-time responsibility of becoming the company's social networking expert. This will likely become part of your job or will be added to the list of priorities of one of your employees.

In addition to time and schedule constraints, companies are increasingly deciding to block employee access to Facebook, Twitter, and LinkedIn via their internal networks. So, if an employee has been assigned the social networking responsibility, how can that person be successful if they have been seemingly handcuffed by being denied access?

Well, the solution for both of these challenges is relatively simple because you will only need to invest about ten minutes a day toward your social networking activities. For example, you will write a status update/post in the morning, respond to any pending messages, write some comments on your friends' walls, and then write your second and final status update/post for the day in the afternoon. All told, you will invest about ten minutes toward these activities and then move on with the rest of your day.

Make two posts per day

You will more than likely quickly determine, as I did, that there are essentially three groups of members within your community, and the groups are defined by the time of day they most frequently access their social networks. The groups are:

1. Morning (6 a.m. to 10 a.m.)
2. Midday (10 a.m. to about 5 p.m.)
3. Evening (5 p.m. to late night)

You will notice some variance with the groups depending on time zones. However, for the most part, the groups will remain intact.

Being aware of this information saves you a ton of valuable time. You can now write just two status updates/posts a day and take advantage of the fact that your community membership is fractured in thirds all the time. The status update/post you write in the morning will essentially cover the morning and midday groups. The status update/post you write in the afternoon will again influence the midday group, as well as the evening crowd.

You should also be aware that you will likely increase your probability of success for increasing online sales if you make your product/service-related posts during the morning time segment. This is a result of the fact that people tend to make online purchases in the morning while at work before their busy day begins. This seems to be especially true for consumer-related products.

I recommend that you take advantage of this by making your product/service-related post while the morning group is more apt to be paying attention to your message. And, because of the 6:1 ratio explained in Step 11, you should make one product/service-related post every three days (6 life/professional-related posts ÷ 2 posts per day = 3 days).

You can save even more time by not investing any time toward your viral social networking strategy during the weekends. It is likely your website traffic from community members will follow the Pareto principle, also known as the 80-20 rule, which says that approximately 80 percent of your website traffic from community members will occur Monday through Friday, while the remaining 20 percent will be over the weekend. This again is directly attributed to the fact that a high percentage of people are actively engaged in social networking activities while at work.

The following is a daily checklist for small business owners and managers that will reduce your time commitment to about ten minutes a day:

❏ Write two new status updates/posts, Tweets, and network updates each day to distribute your content to your community members. One status update/post should be written in the morning and one should be written in the afternoon.

❏ Reply to comments posted by members concerning your previous status updates/posts.

❏ Scan your Facebook news feed and make one comment per day regarding the status update or new photo albums of a friend.

❏ Check your Facebook "Events" section on your Facebook news feed to find the current birthday lists. Then, write birthday wishes to all of your Facebook friends on the day of their birthdays.

❏ Reply to pending inbox, InMail, and direct messages.

Viral Social Networking Checklist: Part 7

❏ Prepare the supporting content page(s) on your website.

❏ Write a life/professional-related post or product/service-related post, embed a link to the supporting content page on your website, and distribute to your community members on Facebook, Twitter, and LinkedIn.

❏ Write six life/professional-related posts for each product/service-related post you write.

❏ Begin building trust by writing comments within 24 hours to any wall postings your community members post on your Facebook wall.

❏ Scan your Facebook news feed, and write comments regarding the status updates of community members or new photo albums that have been posted.

❏ Check your "Events" section for birthdays of community members.

❏ Reply within 24 hours to any comments your community members post regarding your Facebook status updates or LinkedIn network updates.

❏ Reply within 24 hours to any Twitter direct messages you receive.

❏ Begin your march toward ten minutes of social networking a day by writing just two new status updates/posts, Tweets, and network updates per day — one in the morning and one in the afternoon.

❏ Reply to comments posted by members concerning your previous status updates/posts.

❏ Scan your Facebook news feed, and make one comment per day regarding the status update or new photo albums of a friend.

❏ Write birthday wishes to all of your Facebook friends on their birthday.

❏ Reply to pending inbox, InMail, and direct messages.

❏ Proceed to Chapter 8: Boost your social networking efficiency and effectiveness.

Boost Your Social Networking Efficiency and Effectiveness

Viral social networking steps covered in this chapter:

▸ **Step 14:** Use free tools like NutshellMail to save even more time.

One of the common concerns I hear from small business owners or managers about participating in social networking is their perception that the time commitment required will be substantial. It has been my experience in working with small business owners that the common belief is that someone will need to devote many hours toward their social networking strategy every single day in order to be successful. If you are like most people, you likely do not have the luxury of being able to invest a significant amount of time toward a new marketing initiative. Consequently, if your viral social networking strategy is not something you can manage in a few minutes a day or less, it will never get done. There are too many other priorities that require your attention.

The good news is that if you follow the recommendations in Step 13, your social networking participation will never consume your schedule. In fact, your efforts will be easy to manage in about ten minutes a day. And, there is even better news. There a several free social networking tools available that can help you develop even more efficiency to further reduce your time investment.

You may have already heard of, or perhaps already use, some of the more common free social networking tools like Ping.fm (**www.ping.fm**), HootSuite™ (**http://hootsuite.com**), or TweetDeck™ (**www.tweetdeck.com**). I encourage you to consider evaluating each of them. Each tool is robust and includes some excellent features. The downside to each of these tools is that they are comprehensive in scope and ideally suited for someone looking to monitor the hour-by-hour activities taking place within their online brand community.

While most of us would love to have the time to use some of these real-time tools, the reality is that small business owners do not have that much time available in their schedules. From my perspective, there is only one free social networking tool on the market that was designed with the busy owner and manager in mind. The tool is called NutshellMail (**http://nutshellmail.com**), which is owned by Constant Contact. *See Chapter 5 for more information on Constant Contact.*

I am a huge fan of NutshellMail because it is easy to use and saves time. This chapter demonstrates how you can incorporate NutshellMail into your viral social networking strategy with the goal of helping you maximize your efficiency. When developing my plan for the chapter, I decided to reach out to NutshellMail with the hope of being able to interview someone who could provide a true insider perspective about the features and benefits the tool provides small business owners and managers. The company's extremely helpful staff connected me with Mark Schmulen, one of NutshellMail's co-founders. Schmulen became the general manager of social media marketing at Constant Contact following the company's acquisition of NutshellMail.

The beginning of this chapter shares highlights from the insightful conversation I had with Schmulen. These highlights will be followed by Step 14 of the social networking process, which will demonstrate precisely how to get started using NutshellMail.

Interview with Mark Schmulen

One of the main reasons NutshellMail has become so popular is because the tool is easy to use. NutshellMail gives you the ability to manage and coordinate your Facebook, Twitter, and LinkedIn activities much like the other free social networking tools mentioned earlier in this chapter. However, a significant difference between NutshellMail and the other tools is that it is the only one that gives you the ability to manage all of your activity using something you are already familiar with and likely use every day — your e-mail inbox. You simply check your e-mail and manage you social networks. It is that simple!

I enjoyed my interview with Schulmen because he took the time to share NutshellMail's passion for adding value to small business owners. From my perspective, the company really seems to understand the time constraints small business owners are under every day, and I think it is this understanding that motivated the company to create a social networking tool that could be used right away with very little time investment from business owners.

Stephen: Why did you make the e-mail inbox the focal point with NutshellMail?

Mark: Our primary goal was to design a social networking tool with the needs of small business owners and managers in mind. The e-mail inbox has become a real hub of communication for many businesspeople so we thought it would be practical to make the inbox the cornerstone of NutshellMail.

Making things simple was our goal. We believe that asking a businessperson to learn how to use a new software package or destination website would be unrealistic given the constant time constraints, interruptions, and pressures they face. If NutshellMail took too much time to learn or use, our goal of meeting the needs of small business owners and managers would go unmet.

Ultimately, we have given businesspeople a tool that will help them get even more value out of their e-mail inboxes while capitalizing on all of the benefits social networking provides. NutshellMail gives small business owners and busy managers the ability to stay connected with their social networks in significantly less time.

Stephen: How would you summarize what NutshellMail can do for a businessperson?

Mark: Great question. NutshellMail is very similar to a DVR, like many of us have in our homes, which records your television programs and allows you to watch them on your own time. NutshellMail works in a similar way, essentially capturing and recording all of the information and activity from your online brand community. It packages all of your social networking activity into a concise e-mail and delivers it to your inbox on the schedule that you preset.

With NutshellMail, you do not have to spend time monitoring your Facebook, Twitter, or LinkedIn accounts in fear that an important conversation or update will be missed. NutshellMail will capture it all and deliver it to you in one package.

Stephen: You described NutshellMail to me as a time-saving listening tool. What did you mean by that?

Mark: The ability to create a two-way dialogue with customers and prospects is one of the most attractive benefits to using social networking within a business context. Facebook, Twitter, and LinkedIn give us the ability to listen to customers and prospects like never before. NutshellMail extends this a step further by giving you the ability to not only listen but also proactively communicate with customers all from your inbox. This level of engaged communication creates and builds strong relationships within your brand community…all while saving you time.

Stephen: So, NutshellMail has eliminated the need for individual notifications from Facebook, Twitter, and LinkedIn?

Mark: Exactly because NutshellMail will compile all of these notifications into one simple e-mail and deliver it to your inbox as often as you like. Some people want to receive NutshellMail updates every hour. Others choose to have their updates delivered less frequently. The point is that you are in charge and can set your own schedule. And, if you are too busy when the update is delivered to your inbox, you may choose to delete it. Most people choose to receive between two and three NutshellMail updates a day.

Stephen: Is NutshellMail one-size-fits-all or can a businessperson customize their account?

Mark: NutshellMail provides several powerful options for customization that can save you even more time. For example, the typical Facebook member has between 160 to 180 friends. It can take a lot of time to develop engaged relationships with this many people. NutshellMail makes communicating with a large audience more efficient. We provide a person with the ability to create separate lists for different groups of Facebook friends — like customers, prospects, family members, etc. — whose updates you definitely do not want to miss. Then, NutshellMail can be customized to only deliver updates related to those lists. You will not be distracted by updates from people who are not members of the lists you created.

NutshellMail also makes Twitter more user friendly and valuable. First, NutshellMail can be customized so that it informs you not only when you have a new Twitter follower but also when someone decides to unfollow you. NutshellMail will also inform you when a direct message has been received or when anyone on Twitter mentions you. In addition, NutshellMail can also alert you based on keywords. This gives you the ability to effectively monitor your industry, competitors, customers, or any other relevant topic.

In effect, NutshellMail is like a person's social networking RSS reader because it can be used it to filter out all of the noise. You can keep track of everything you want…and nothing you don't.

Stephen: What are some of the new developments with NutshellMail?

Mark: We are constantly working on new and interesting projects. One of our latest developments is that we now provide the ability to manage both your personal and business Facebook profiles via your inbox. We are also working on an integration project with YouTube.

We have also accomplished some outstanding integrations of social networking into our Constant Contact product. Here is a tangible example that illustrates the recommendations you made during Chapter 5 of your book, which demonstrates the power of e-mail and social networking being integrated. One of our Constant Contact customers recently sent an e-mail campaign to 3,700 customers and prospects. The company experienced a 21.6 percent open rate with approximately 800 people reading it. However, the company was smart to choose to use our sharing features, which allow you to easily integrate social media icons into your e-mail, making the content very easy for the recipients to share socially. The results were that an additional 485 people viewed the e-mail campaign. This viral aspect of social networking extended the reach of the original e-mail campaign by 60 percent. Incredible results!

Step 14: Use Free Tools like NutshellMail to Save Even More Time

Are you ready to begin using NutshellMail to make your social networking strategy even more efficient? Open any Web browser and visit the company's website at **http://nutshellmail.com**. You will likely see a NutshellMail home page that looks similar to the one shown in Figure 8.1.

Figure 8.1 NutshellMail welcome screen

© 2010 NutshellMail

Creating a NutshellMail account is simple and only takes a couple minutes. Click the "Create an Account" link that is displayed in the upper right corner of the screen shot shown in Figure 8.1. When you click the link, you will receive a screen that looks similar to the screen shot shown in Figure 8.2. This is the NutshellMail account application.

Figure 8.2 Steps 1 and 2 of the account creation process

© 2010 NutshellMail

Begin by providing NutshellMail with the e-mail address you would like to associate with your account. You should also create a password. Once you have entered the information into these fields, you will need to complete Step 2 of the process, which consists of connecting your NutshellMail account with your social network accounts, such as Facebook, Twitter, LinkedIn, and/or MySpace. NutshellMail requires you to connect at least one of your social network accounts to your NutshellMail account or the signup process cannot be completed. For the purpose of illustrating this process, I selected Twitter as the social networking account to connect to NutshellMail. It does not matter which social networking site you connect NutshellMail with first. You can always add more later.

We will assume you decided to connect your Twitter account first. After clicking on the Twitter logo, you will receive a screen that likely looks similar to the screenshot shown in Figure 8.3. Twitter will prompt you to enter your Twitter account information, which will then be passed to NutshellMail in order to complete the connection process.

Figure 8.3 Linking NutshellMail with your social accounts

© 2010 NutshellMail
© 2010 Twitter

You can then repeat the same steps to connect your Facebook and LinkedIn accounts to NutshellMail. You will receive a screen that likely looks similar to the screenshot shown Figure 8.4 once all of your social networking accounts have been connected.

You will use this screen to manage and customize all of the social networking accounts that are connected to your NutshellMail account. For example, within Figure 8.4, you can see that my NutshellMail account is currently connected to my Facebook, Twitter, LinkedIn, and my "seotrainingproducts" YouTube channel. To customize NutshellMail for Facebook, I simply click on the gray "Customize" link to the far right of the Facebook logo on this screen. NutshellMail will then give you a screen that likely looks similar to the screenshot shown in Figure 8.5.

Figure 8.4 Add/manage your accounts

© 2010 NutshellMail

The "Customize Your Facebook Account" screen gives you many options to consider. The "Include" checkboxes on the left allow you to select or de-select whether you want these Facebook updates included in your e-mail updates from NutshellMail. Check the box to the left of the "Inbox Messages" option if you want your Facebook messages included within your NutshellMail e-mail update, and then proceed down the list. As you can see from this screenshot, I decided to include Facebook messages, notifications, tagged photos, birthdays, friend requests, wall posts, and thread posts in my NutshellMail e-mail updates.

I could then go to Facebook and change my settings to turn off the e-mails I would have normally received from Facebook notifying me of these items. This greatly reduces my inbox clutter and saves me time because I am now getting all of my Facebook updates in one e-mail from NutshellMail instead of many sporadic e-mails throughout the day from Facebook.

In addition, NutshellMail also gives you the option to select the number of messages, notifications, etc. you would like to have included within your NutshellMail updates. The quantities that are shown in Figure 8.5 are the default settings.

Then, click the gray "Save" button when you are finished customizing your Facebook settings. Now, repeat this customization process for your Twitter and LinkedIn accounts to get the most time saving efficiency out of NutshellMail.

Figure 8.5 Customize each of your social network accounts

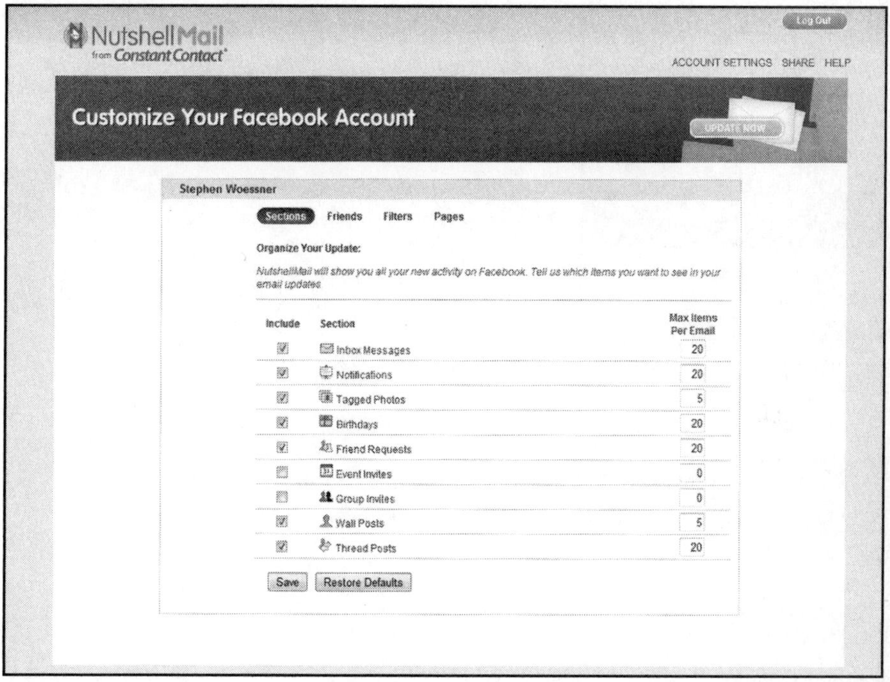

© 2010 NutshellMail

There is one final step to configuring your NutshellMail account, which involves setting the schedule for when you would like NutshellMail to e-mail the updates to your inbox. To set the schedule, you need to click on the "Delivery Times" link located within the "Account Settings" menu on the left side of the NutshellMail screen. The "Account Settings" menu will likely look similar to the screenshot shown in Figure 8.6.

Figure 8.6 Your account settings

© 2010 NutshellMail

NutshellMail will then give you a screen that looks similar to Figure 8.7. The first option in the delivery schedule is the day-of-week option. I recommend that you select the Monday through Friday options and leave Saturday and Sunday unchecked. I recommend this because your opportunity for generating website traffic and online sales on the weekend is greatly reduced because the majority of people participate in social networking during the normal workweek. Take this opportunity to further reduce inbox clutter and your time commitment.

Figure 8.7 Select a delivery schedule that is convenient for you

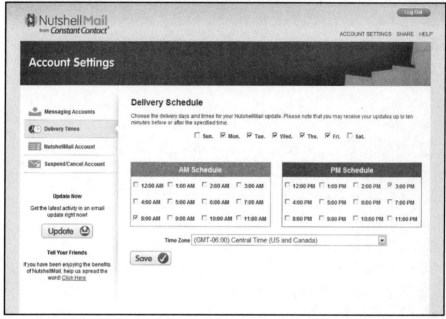

© 2010 NutshellMail

Next, you will need to select your "AM Schedule" and "PM Schedule." You can see from the options in Figure 8.7 that NutshellMail has made hourly updates an option for you to consider. I have experimented with multiple variations in scheduling, and in my opinion, the most efficient and effective is selecting 8 a.m. and again 3 p.m. This keeps my time commitment to a minimum, but it still gives me all of the important information I need to review on a daily basis.

Just like a dinner recipe, the individual ingredients or steps in the viral social networking process when implemented in unison will produce powerful results. Likewise, when you blend Steps 13 and 14 together, you will generate significant results in ten minutes a day. When I developed this process, I felt it was critical to condense it into a series of steps you as a business owner or manager could realistically fit into your schedules. I hope you think I accomplished that goal now that you have studied the first 14 steps in the 15-step process. The final step in the process is all about measuring your results!

Viral Social Networking Checklist: Part 8

❏ Open any Web browser and go to the NutshellMail website (**http://nutshellmail.com**) to create your free account.

❏ Connect your Facebook, Twitter, and LinkedIn accounts to your NutshellMail account.

❏ Customize your NutshellMail account settings for your Facebook, Twitter, and LinkedIn accounts.

❏ Use the Account Settings menu to customize your NutshellMail "Delivery Schedule."

❏ Proceed to Chapter 9: Measuring Your Results.

Measuring Your Results

Viral social networking steps covered in this chapter:

▶ **Step 15:** Install and use Google Analytics to track and measure your viral social networking results.

The final step in the viral social networking process focuses solely on providing you with what you need to be able to efficiently and effectively measure your results. As stated earlier in this book, you will likely increase your website traffic by approximately 23 percent through a combination of Facebook, Twitter, and LinkedIn. Step 15 will show you how to install and use Google Analytics as the cornerstone of your measurement toolbox.

Part 1 of this chapter will show you how to install Google Analytics on your website so you can begin collecting data. Please proceed to Part 2 of this chapter if you are already using Google Analytics.

Part 2 will show you how to use the reports provided within Google Analytics to determine how much of your website traffic is being generated by your online brand community members. In addition,

Google Analytics can be used to drill down to individual website content pages so you can evaluate the success of the social networking posts that you wrote and distributed during Steps 7 and 10 of this process.

There is one thing to keep in mind before reviewing Parts 1 and 2. As you begin evaluating your results via Google Analytics, you will notice spikes and valleys to your website traffic similar to the screenshot shown in Figure 9.1.

Figure 9.1 Google Analytics dashboard view of site visits

©2010 Google

The spikes within your Google Analytics data will likely synchronize with the dates you distributed social networking posts that included links back to your website content. The decreases or valleys within your Google Analytics data will likely synchronize with the days where you did not make social networking posts. I am confident you will experience measurable results that help you arrive at the same conclusion I have: Social networking activity quantifiably increases website traffic and online sales. The reverse is also true. Decreases in social networking activity results in a reduction of website traffic and online sales.

Step 15: Install and use Google Analytics to Track and Measure Your Viral Social Networking Results

Part 1: Install Google Analytics

I also recommended the section on installation of Google Analytics that can be found in my book, *The Small Business Owner's Handbook to Search Engine*

Optimization. The process of installation has not changed so I decided to pull in an excerpt from the "SEO Quick Start Guide" found in Chapter 2 of the book.

"Google describes Google Analytics as a free Web-based application that provides data regarding the path visitors used to find a website (i.e. search engine, referred by another website, etc.), the most popular content within the website, the number of unique visitors, site visits, and a variety of other variables. Theoretically, a website owner can use this information to enhance his or her website and increase the conversion rate of online sales.

Google defines unique visitors (or absolute unique visitors) as the number of unduplicated (counted only once) visitors to a website over the course of a specified time, typically 30 days. Google Analytics also measures site visits and visitors to a website. Site visits represent the number of individual sessions initiated by all the visitors to a website. If a user is inactive on a website for 30 minutes or more, any future activity will be attributed to a new session. Users who leave a website and return within 30 minutes will be counted as part of the original session. The initial session by a user during any given date range is considered to be an additional visit and an additional visitor. Any future sessions from the same user during the selected time period are counted as additional visits, but they are not counted as additional visitors.

Google Analytics is a free service that has replaced the need for small business owners to invest any additional money toward high-quality traffic statistics in order to understand how their website is performing and which keywords are delivering the most traffic. Granted, if your website is hosted by a quality company, they likely provide some level of statistics as part of their package. However, Google Analytics tends to provide data that is more comprehensive. Plus, it is fully integrated with Google AdWords, in case you ever decide to launch a pay-per-click advertising campaign to further boost your site traffic.

Click on the blue 'Access Analytics' button from the Google Analytics home page (**www.google.com/analytics**), as shown in Figure 9.2, or click the 'Sign Up Now' link, if you do not have a Google account. Once you create an account with Google, you will be able to use the same username and password for Analytics, AdWords, Webmaster Tools, and a variety of other Google features.

Figure 9.2 Google Analytics welcome screen

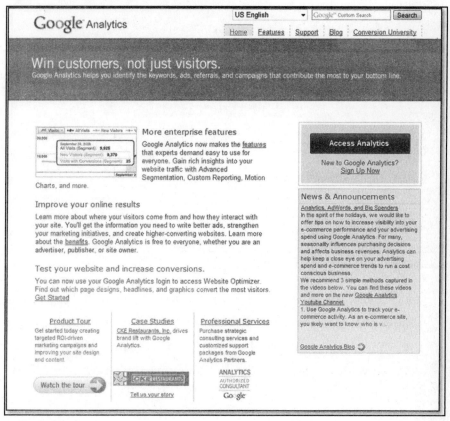

©2010 Google

Once signed in, you will be prompted to create a Google Analytics account. Click on the 'Sign Up' button within the box titled 'Sign up for Google Analytics' shown in Figure 9.3. You will then be asked to enter some basic information about you and your website. This information is used to create your customized 'Tracking Code.'

Figure 9.3 Sign up here

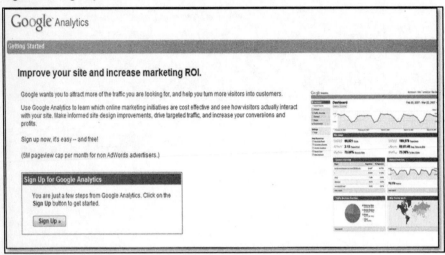

©2010 Google

Your customized Google Analytics Tracking Code will appear in a window that looks similar to the screenshot in Figure 9.4. Your next step is to copy and paste the tracking code into every page of your website that you want to have tracked. The code must be pasted immediately before the </body> tag.

Figure 9.4 Your tracking code instructions

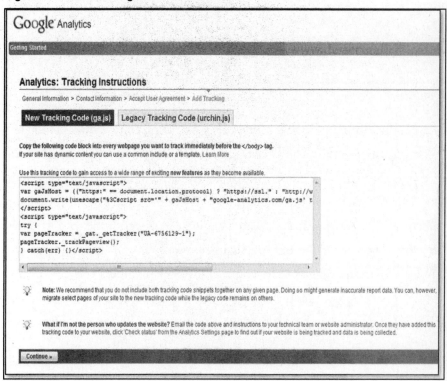

©2010 Google

You can also open a Web browser and go to **www.google.com/support/ googleanalytics** if you have additional questions or concerns regarding how or where to paste the tracking code."

Part 2: Measuring social networking effectiveness

Google Analytics will provide you with a "Dashboard" view of your most recent 30 days of website traffic when you log in to your Analytics account. You can customize the time you would like to analyze by clicking on the dates displayed in the upper right corner of the Google Analytics window as shown in Figure 9.5.

Figure 9.5 Dashboard view of site visits

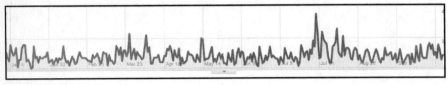

©2010 Google

The "Traffic Sources Overview" report is one of the most valuable default reports featured within the Dashboard. It can be found in the bottom left of the Dashboard and looks similar to the screen shot shown in Figure 9.6. This overview combines the individual traffic sources into four main categories: 1) referring sites, 2) search engines, 3) direct traffic, and 4) other. The referring sites is the one that will be more closely examined because any website traffic generated by your community members will be reported within this category. Google Analytics allows you to drill down further to see more granular data by clicking the "View report" link in the lower left.

Figure 9.6 Dashboard view of traffic sources

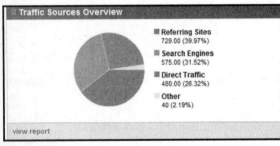

©2010 Google

Clicking on the "View report" link will provide you with a report that looks similar to the screen shot shown in Figure 9.7. The "Top Traffic Sources" report shows that Google's organic search results represented 26.86 percent of total site visits. More interestingly, Twitter followers represented 11.02 percent of total site visits, while Facebook friends represented 9.98

percent. Although not shown on the summary report, LinkedIn represented approximately 4 percent of total site visits. The total site visits statistics is a summation of all visits to all content pages found within the website.

Figure 9.7 Detailed view of traffic sources

Top Traffic Sources		
Sources	Visits	% visits
google (organic)	490	26.86%
(direct) ((none))	480	26.32%
twitter.com (referral)	20˙	11.02%
facebook.com (referral)	182	9.98%
google (cpc)	73	4.00%
view full report		

©2010 Google

This aggregate information is helpful so you can evaluate how your social networking activity affects total site traffic. But, it would also be helpful to evaluate the results delivered by each of your social networking posts as they relate to a specific content page within your website. Google Analytics provides you with that capability, which can be accessed by clicking on the gray "Content" link within the left side menu shown in Figure 9.8.

Figure 9.8 Navigation and menu options

©2010 Google

Google Analytics will now deliver a "Content Overview" Dashboard. Direct your attention to the lower left of this Dashboard in order to locate the "Top Content" report that will look similar to the screenshot shown in Figure 9.9. This summary report shows the specific percentage of page views generated by individual content pages. The first content page listed in the summary is identified by a backslash symbol of (/). The backslash is always used to represent the website's home page. Therefore, Google Analytics has determined that the home page received 22.13 percent of the site's total page views.

Figure 9.9 Top content summary report

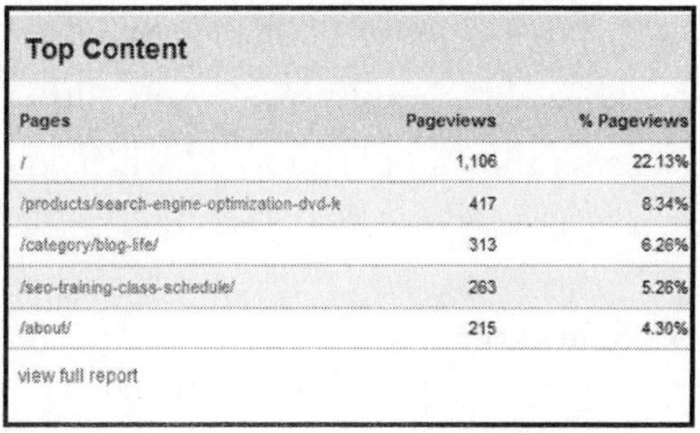

Top Content		
Pages	Pageviews	% Pageviews
/	1,106	22.13%
/products/search-engine-optimization-dvd-k	417	8.34%
/category/blog-life/	313	6.26%
/seo-training-class-schedule/	263	5.26%
/about/	215	4.30%
view full report		

©2010 Google

Although this is good information, it does not provide the specific information necessary to evaluate your social networking efforts. Therefore, we need to dig deeper in Google Analytics by clicking on one of the "Pages" links within the "Top Content" report. Regardless of which content page link you choose to click, you will receive another Dashboard view that will provide you with traffic data related to only the particular page you selected. Within the bottom right of the Dashboard view, you will see a menu of additional data analysis tools that looks similar to the screenshot shown in Figure 9.10.

Figure 9.10 Select "entrance sources"

Navigation Analysis

Navigation Summary
How visitors found your content

Entrance Paths
Paths visitors used to get to your content

Landing Page Optimization

Entrance Sources
Top sources per page

Entrance Keywords
Top keywords per page

Click Patterns

In-Page Analytics Beta
Click data on top of your website

©2010 Google

The "Entrance Sources" tool within the "Landing Page Optimization" section will provide you with the precise social networking data you need to evaluate your effectiveness. Google Analytics will provide you with a report that looks similar to the screenshot shown in Figure 9.11 when you click on "Entrance Sources."

Figure 9.11 Top entrance sources or referring sites

	Source	None ⌄	Pageviews ↓
1.	(direct)		2,788
2.	google		1,534
3.	twitter.com		678
4.	facebook.com		400
5.	74.125.47.132		255
6.	uwlax.edu		123
7.	youtube.com		77
8.	linkedin.com		74
9.	myseoindia.com		47
10.	bernadot.com		28

©2010 Google

This report shows that the page being reviewed received 678 total pageviews from Twitter. The earlier Dashboard also reported total pageviews for this content page at 2,542. With some quick division, divide 678 by 2,542 to calculate the total number of pageviews that Twitter followers were responsible for generating. In this example, that number is an astounding 26.6 percent.

However, it is important to recognize that the above numbers represent a comprehensive summary of all pageviews generated by this one content page over the life of the content page. In order to evaluate the impact of a specific social networking post for a specific content page, simply adjust the dates

Viral Social Networking Checklist: Part 9

❏ Create your free Google account so you can take advantage of Google Analytics.

❏ Create a Google Analytics account and install tracking code into your website.

❏ Log in to your Google Analytics report to review your main Dashboard of statistics.

❏ Click on the "View Report" link beneath the "Traffic Sources Overview" Dashboard to view site specific data.

❏ Click on the "Content" link in left side menu of Google Analytics in order to review social networking data that is page specific.

❏ Click on any of the "Pages" links within the "Top Content" summary report.

❏ Click on the "Entrance Sources" tool within the "Landing Page Optimization" section.

❏ Evaluate the effectiveness of a specific social networking post by adjusting the date(s) in the upper right of your Google Analytics screen so they match your posting date.

❏ Proceed to Chapter 10: Putting it All Together.

CHAPTER 10:

Pulling it All Together

Business owners and marketing managers frequently ask me questions about how to generate results from their social networking participation. Their questions tend to revolve around three main categories: 1) how to get started, 2) will their results be tangible, and 3) will social networking actually be worth their time investment? As I prepared to conclude this book, I made the assumption that there a lot of people out there, and maybe even you, who share the same questions or concerns. This is why I added this special section — to address frequently asked questions (FAQs).

Another reason FAQs are so helpful is that they often help us relate to the problem that the person asking the question is trying to solve because we are likely dealing with the same issue. Because of this, I wanted to take this chapter a bit further by also including three success stories regarding small business owners who have benefited from their use of social networking to promote what they do.

Frequently Asked Questions about Viral Social Networking

The following are 14 of the most frequently asked questions I am asked by small business owners and managers about social networking. You will see that their concerns range from time investment to results. I hope you find the FAQs to be insightful.

I also recommend you visit the Power to the Small Business website (**www. powertothesmallbusiness.com/2010/08/social-media-marketing-for-mula-sales-conversion**). The website contains a podcast of an interview I did with Jay Ehret who runs The Marketing Spot (**www.themarketingspot. com**), a small business consulting firm in Texas. I decided to share several of his questions in this chapter because I think they precisely address the core issues important to business owners. You can learn more about Jay Ehret by reading the social networking success story later in this chapter.

Q1: I have heard social networking described as part of the new "trust economy." What does that mean?

A: Trust is so critically important and is the basis of all our interpersonal relationships. Without trust, relationships are not relationships at all. They are more like casual acquaintances. I believe that the line between business and personal relationships has blurred and people are more interested in doing business with people than ever before. Social networking helps facilitate these types of interpersonal relationships, and trust can absolutely be built. With trust, tie strength develops and an online brand community is formed. It all begins with trust because people do not buy something from someone they do not trust.

Q2: What advice do you have for business owners who are looking to sell products or services to the members of their online brand community?

A: Great question. I think that this one also connects back to trust. We have to be genuine with the content and communication we share with our online brand community. Being fake or disingenuous for the purpose of profit is very easy to spot, and when it is spotted, people will quickly tune out or abandon the community all together because it no longer provides value. I think best-selling author and marketing guru Seth Godin had it right when he said, "Social networking is always important when it is real and is always a useless distraction when it is fake." My advice is to always be genuine…never be fake.

Q3: Why is having a plan with specific goals so important?

A: Well, it is like that age-old adage: "If you do not have goals or a destination in mind, what difference does it make what direction you go?" The same is true for social networking. Business owners need to think strategically about whether they will be building the brand of their business with their viral social networking activities or if they will work to build a personal profile (brand). Trust has been easier to build when a business owner has developed his or her own personal brand versus creating "Like" pages on Facebook.

People develop and build deep levels of trust with other people and not companies or corporate brands. We have all probably been back to a store or restaurant specifically because there was a person working there who took exceptional care of our needs so we felt compelled to do business there again. I think it makes sense for a business owner to set the goal of building a personal profile (brand) through his or her viral social networking activities in order to create trusting relationships with customers and prospects. However, the overall key is to have a plan with tangible goals. Some goals to consider could be an increase in unique website visitors from X to X, an increase in online sales from X to X, an increase in the length of session visits, or an increase in the number of e-newsletter subscribers.

Q4: What advice would you share with the business owner who considers social networking to be overwhelming and does not know where to start?

A: Take small steps, and do not worry about making mistakes. It is highly unlikely that once a person creates his or her Facebook account that he or she will turn into an overnight sensation. Begin to find interesting people who you already know on Facebook, Twitter, and LinkedIn, and invite them to join your community. Then, develop some experience in creating quality content and sharing the content with members of their community. And finally, communicate frequently while keeping the overall goals in mind. Initiating communication with members of your community by making status updates or sharing content twice per day is ideal.

Q5: What is the best way for someone to measure success with viral social networking?

A: The true measurement for any business owner is at the cash register. If sales are up, then the viral social networking efforts are likely producing results. Being able to measure results is one of the reasons why social networking is a terrific promotional tool, and Google Analytics makes the measurement process easy and straightforward.

Q6: How many Facebook photo albums should I have within my profile?

A: I do not think there is a magic number. The Facebook photo albums will not directly drive traffic to your business website per se. The Facebook albums will let your community members into aspects of your life to further develop relationships. The albums should be used to highlight aspects of your life that you want to share, i.e. vacations, birthdays, and other special events. There is no need to feel pressure to upload a new Facebook album every week.

I think a good rule of thumb to follow may be to add one album per month in order to keep your community members actively engaged. You are likely adding too many photos to Facebook if you begin creating things to do for the primary purpose of shooting photos you can add to your albums. Take a break if you find yourself in this situation, and go back to one album a month.

Q7: Why do some of the tactics within Step 5 of your social networking process seem to be passive versus proactive?

A: Good question. While some of the tactics are passive, they are also foundational. For example, suppose you decided to send the e-mail campaign recommended within tactic No. 4 to your customers and prospects before you added the social networking logos or orientation content pages to your website. You would have to rely on the generic welcome pages of the social networking sites as the destination from the e-mail campaign.

What if one of your customers or prospects has a question as a result of receiving the e-mail campaign and they send you an e-mail? This is an ideal next step because it establishes a communication channel and gives you an opportunity to solve a prospective customer's problem and hopefully instill the confidence necessary to close a sale. It would be a missed opportunity if your signature at the end of your e-mail does not include links to your social networking orientation content pages on your website.

These are just a few examples that illustrate the need for the foundational content to be developed first before proactive promotional tactics are incorporated into the mix.

Q8: How did you discover the 6:1 ratio that you recommended in Chapter 7?

A: I wish my answer could be something more impressive than just trial and error, but unfortunately, that is how the ratio started. I experimented with several different ratios. Some were pro-commerce, meaning that I was making social networking posts regarding products and services much more often than every third day. I also experimented with less frequent messages, which placed a greater emphasis on life/professional-related posts. But, when I went back and reviewed the data, the ratio that produced the most website traffic and online sales was the 6:1 ratio. Again, nothing fancy…just plain old data analysis.

Q9: How long will it take a person to set up his or her Facebook, Twitter, and LinkedIn communities and grow them to the point that commerce can happen?

A: It is realistic for a businessperson to expect about a 90-day setup time. This includes the time necessary to become familiar with Facebook, Twitter, and LinkedIn. The 90 days also includes the time involved with implementing the checklists found in Chapters 5 and 6. This will ensure that a solid foundation of conversation has begun and the business's website has the supporting content. Then, it is time to begin distributing content as part of Step 10 in the process and measure the results.

Q10: Should I invest in building my online brand community around a personal profile or a business profile?

A: This is an excellent question, and there are several trade-offs to consider with each. If you develop your brand around your personal profile, I believe you are more likely to establish credibility and build relationships that are built on trust. I believe this because your community members will communicate directly with you versus an impersonal business profile. However, I have seen some small business owners pull off communicating personally through their business Facebook page very well. Mark Harrell, owner of Bad Axe Tool Works who was featured in Chapter 5, is an excellent example. The downside to the personal profile is that Facebook limits you to 5,000 friends.

The advantages to having a Facebook page for your business is that the content you post can be indexed by search engines because normally the privacy settings are open. You are not limited to 5,000 friends — there is no limit to the number of people who can "Like" you. However, with a Facebook page, you cannot send out "Like" invitations as you can send out Friend Requests within your personal profile.

Ultimately, a business owner must decide which direction is the best fit for his or her strategy. I have met some business owners who maintain a personal and business profile on Facebook. This is a good strategy if a person has the necessary time.

Q11: How did you encourage your social networking members to make purchases?

A: I never said, "Buy this product or that product." I did not have to. The content spoke for itself. I think one thing that cannot be overstated is the need to be genuine — do not try to sell all the time. Avoid the temptation to turn your online community into a selling free-for-all. Conversation and community must be established before commerce can take place. Once all of these building place are established, sharing your content, as outlined in Step 10 of the process, will deliver excellent results.

Q12: What kind of personal posts are appropriate for a business?

A: The list of topics is nearly endless. A person could write posts that highlight new employees, birthday parties in the office, company picnics, and recent trade shows where the company exhibited. You could also post photos of company representatives giving speeches in the community or during industry events. Any combination of these types of posts will help customers and prospects feel they are getting a behind-the-scenes look into your company and the lives of its employees. All of this develops trusts and strengthens relationships because people enjoy doing business with people they like, and what is a company other than a collection of people.

Q13: How long can sales from social networking activity be sustainable? Do business owners have to continually look for new friends, followers, and connections?

A: The results from a social networking post are nearly instantaneous. A business owner will likely notice an increase in website traffic and online sales within minutes of informing community members that a particular content page was available. But, the results are relatively short-lived. It has been my experience that spikes in traffic and online sales wane approximately 72 hours following the social networking post.

In addition, yes, the process of expanding your sphere of influence, as outlined in Chapter 5, should be ongoing. Your community needs to continually expand. The more members and conversations, the more trust is built, and as your community grows larger, your credibility within your industry increases — all of which can have a positive effect on sales.

Q14: Do you get tired or burnt out from all of the social networking activity?

A: I have at times, yes. Social networking is just like anything else in life. Sometimes, we need to take a break and come back to it after we have had a chance to re-energize. When I take vacations, I tend to not use Facebook, Twitter, or LinkedIn. This gives me a couple of weeks to mentally tune out and collect my thoughts. When my vacation time is over, I come back and begin sharing my experiences and photos from the trip. For me, this has been a good balance, but everyone has different needs for what they feel is the right balance.

Small Business Success Stories

Throughout this book, I referenced aspects of what was learned during the launch of my website as part of a comprehensive research study. However, I tried to limit the detail that was shared earlier in order to provide a high-level view of the study. I wanted the emphasis of the earlier chapters in this book to be about results and the how-to steps of the social networking process versus being bogged down in research and data points. But, for some readers, learning more about the research that helped shaped the 15-step process might be valuable. That is why I decided to include a bit more detail from the study within the success stories shared in this chapter.

I have also included the success stories of two other small business owners who have efficiently and effectively used viral social networking to create conversation, build a brand community, and generate commerce.

Lastly, I would like to make you an offer. I am currently working on the draft of my third book, which will focus on the topic of integrated online marketing, such as blending SEO strategies with social networking, e-mail marketing, content development, pay-per-click advertising, and more. I also plan to dedicate at least a full chapter to small business owner success stories.

That's where the offer comes in. I am in search of small business owners who have experienced success using integrated online marketing and are willing to share their stories with readers around the world. If that sounds like you, and you are interested in being considered, please e-mail me some details about your story at **info@seotrainingproducts.com**. I look forward to hearing from you!

Success story No. 1: SEOTrainingProducts.com

STP or STP.com within the following success story refers to **www.seotrainingproducts.com**.

STP launched on June 21, 2009. Visitors to STP could access articles, download search engine optimization (SEO) tools, or read blog postings written by me. STP launched with the goal of promoting my first book, *The Small Business Owner's Handbook to Search Engine Optimization.*

STP visitors interested in buying a copy of the book, along with its companion DVD learning series, can complete their orders via the STP shopping cart. Or, if an STP visitor only wants to purchase the book, the website contains links to Amazon.com so the customer can order the book. STP's online sales consists of three order variations: 1) DVD learning series only, 2) DVD Learning Series plus the book combo, and 3) book only. All DVD-related orders are fulfilled by STP, while all book-only orders are fulfilled by Amazon. com. All links to Amazon.com contain STP's affiliate tracking code so the referral traffic can be measured and later analyzed.

STP is the exclusive source for purchasing the DVD learning series. However, STP is not the only source customers can use to purchase the book. In addition to visiting Amazon.com without ever having passed through STP, customers can purchase the book via Barnesandnoble.com, Borders.com, Target.com, and other online retailers, including directly from the publisher's website at **www.atlantic-pub.com**. The book is also available at Barnes & Noble retail stores and libraries across the United States. Lastly, the book is available internationally via Amazon.com in the United Kingdom, France, Germany, Japan, and Canada.

I have constructed my online brand community using the three leading social networking sites: Facebook, Twitter, and LinkedIn. This construction began approximately 90 days prior to the launch of the STP website.

The word-of-mouth communications that took place within the online brand community before and after the launch of STP revolved around life/professional-related interests or product-related interests (the book or DVD). I used a combination of embedding links to STP content within the social networking posts, as well as simply writing text-only posts if the context was less formal. Community members clicked on the embedded links within the social networking posts, which directed them to the associated STP website content page(s). Each of these clicks was recorded as referred traffic from whichever social network was the site of origin and then quantifiably tracked using Google Analytics.

I embedded the Amazon.com affiliate links, or links to STP products, within the STP content pages that were announced via my social networking posts. If visitors clicked on the related links, the data was recorded by either Amazon. com or Google Analytics. The data was collected and used to calculate STP's online sales conversion rate.

During the 150 days of data collection (June 21, 2009 to November 17, 2009), I wrote a total of 336 social networking posts, or an average of 2.24 posts per day. STP experienced 78 percent of its traffic during Monday through Friday. The remaining 22 percent of the site traffic occurred Saturday through Sunday. Lastly, 96 percent of the total orders were received Monday through Friday. Only four percent of orders were received during Saturday and Sunday. This seems to indicate that shopping online during normal business hours is prevalent.

I typically wrote social networking posts on an array of topics that might have seemed relevant on a particular day. There was no pre-planning that involved specifying the topic(s). In general, the topic selection was seemingly random. If something occurred during any given day that seemed to be relevant regarding the book, or interesting from a life-professional perspective, then I wrote and distributed a social networking post.

For example, I taught a half-day search engine optimization class at Kent State University-Stark located in North Canton, Ohio. The program was attended by small business owners and managers from the region. Immediately following the completion of the class, I wrote a blog post regarding the experience of teaching the class and then posted the content on STP. The blog post contained one Amazon.com affiliate link so that any clicks to review or order the book online could be tracked. Figure 10.1 is a screen shot of the actual blog post.

Figure 10.1 Blog post example

Taught Search Engine Optimization Class At Kent State University–Stark

The next stop on my book tour to promote *The Small Business Owner's Handbook to Search Engine Optimization* was to teach one of my half-day **search engine optimization classes** at Kent State University-Stark. What an amazing experience!

The participants who attend my search engine optimization classes typically are business owners or managers, or soon-to-be business owners. So the efficiency and effectiveness of my 15-step search engine optimization process was perfect for this group because they don't have the time or money to invest toward things that don't work and produce measurable results. And I will never suggest a business owner invest their resources toward something that isn't proven, which is why I guarantee a person's results when they implement my 15-steps. I get positive feedback all the time, and business owners are impressed with how easy search engine optimization is when they focus on what works and forget the rest.

And the Kent State conference center is easily one of the best facilities I have ever been in. It is unreal. The Kent State staff members lovingly refer to their facility as "The Palace" and I can see why. Every room is any instructor's dream and the catering is impeccable. Today's participants were treated to breakfast including fresh fruit, waffles, and a vast coffee bar. And lunch was even more impressive...a buffet that included cocktail shrimp, salad bar, two different entrees, and desserts galore! It was an amazing experience. And Willie Shoemaker and Jeanne Cramer (left to right) from Kent State were so hospitable. I hope I am invited back because I would accept in an instant!

During the class, I demonstrated each of the 15-steps to my SEO process. The really great thing about the live **search engine optimization classes** is that it gives me the opportunity to use real, tangible examples from the business owners to answer questions or to illustrate points. For example, I used two of the Web sites from a couple of the owners in attendance to demonstrate three of the steps in the SEO process and we actually researched several of the keywords relevant to their business. This is a great hands-on process that is only possible in real-time and this typically exceeds participant's expectations...and I enjoy making the classes as practical and tactical as possible.

All in all, it was a great day! And then my publisher let me know that they were going to do a national media campaign on the book's behalf to schedule some additional interviews and exposure. *The Small Business Owner's Handbook to Search Engine Optimization* has sold out three times in the last four weeks on Amazon! Hopefully this is an indication of really good things to come. Check out the full schedule of my upcoming search engine optimization classes.

Can't attend any of the live search engine optimization classes? Order your copy of the DVD Learning Series and *The Small Business Owner's Handbook to Search Engine Optimization.*

Two affiliate links for the book were embedded within the KSU blog post so clicks to purchase the book off Amazon.com could be tracked. Once the content page was uploaded to STP, I distributed the content via the online brand community. Community members who were interested in the content clicked on the link and were taken to the page on STP so they could read the content. This process was repeated throughout the data collection period.

Throughout the data collection period, absolute unique visitors represented 84.60 percent of total site visits. Twitter and Facebook represented the No. 3 and 4 most productive source/medium of directing traffic to STP. A final point of interest is the percentage of new visits generated by each source/medium. Only 10.45 percent of STP visitors sent from Twitter were new visitors to STP. However, 57.69 percent of STP visitors sent from Facebook were new visitors. Although not conclusive, this is likely because my online community experienced the greatest growth in social network membership on Facebook.

Facebook produced 9.90 percent of the total STP traffic. Twitter was the most effective at referring traffic to STP by producing 11.02 percent of total traffic. LinkedIn represented approximately 4 percent. Cumulatively, referred traffic from Facebook, Twitter, and LinkedIn represented approximately 23 percent of the total site visits. Total traffic from referred sites represented 39.97 percent. Referred traffic from Facebook, Twitter, and LinkedIn represented 52.53 percent of all traffic from referring sites.

The ability for social networking activity to increase STP's traffic by 23 percent or more was impressive. However, the most impressive result was social networking's impact on STP's conversion rate of online sales. Typically, the average e-commerce website will convert between 2 to 4 percent of its unique visitors into buyers. So, for every 100 customers that visit the website, between two and four of them will place an order. However, when the website traffic is comprised of members from a business owner's online brand community, the conversion rate increased up to 22 percent. This represents a 780 percent increase and is directly attributable to the relationship between the community member and business owner. Trust is present, and because people tend to choose to do business with people they like, a higher percentage of conversions take place.

Success story No. 2: Jay Ehret, owner of The Marketing Spot

www.themarketingspot.com

Jay Ehret began his marketing career selling and producing radio advertising for 17 years. Ehret is now a small business marketing consultant, coach, speaker, blog author, and an advertising strategist. He is the chief steward of The Marketing Spot, a company he founded in 2001. The Marketing Spot is located in Waco, Texas.

Ehret and I spent some time talking upon his return from the Blog World and New Media Expo (**www.blogworldexpo.com**) held in Las Vegas. I wanted to know what role, if any, social networking had played in helping him efficiently and effectively build The Marketing Spot's business.

Ehret launched The Marketing Spot's website in October 2001. He launched his blog in March 2007 and his podcasts in December that same year. Ehret has been actively blogging and producing podcasts ever since because he believes both are effective tools for distributing content to a loyal base of clients and prospects. The podcasts are of live interviews he conducts with other marketing experts on a variety of topics. Ehret is an ex-radio station personality and has a terrific voice. He is also comfortable behind a microphone, which makes recording podcasts easy for him to do.

He typically interviews a guest for his show, writes a blog post that summarizes the context of the interview, and then edits and produces the recorded interview into a podcast. On average, he produces at least two podcasts per month. He then announces the availability of his latest podcasts to his Twitter followers and Facebook friends.

Ehret's strategy has been to never overtly sell The Marketing Spot's services within a podcast. His goal has been to focus on sharing the expertise of his guests with his clients and prospects. He believes that this strategy provides his listeners with value and also enhances his credibility in the minds of his listeners.

An additional benefit to producing the podcasts is they have opened a tremendous number of doors for Ehret. He has been able to interview just about any industry expert he chooses. In fact, he has only been turned down twice when approaching someone to interview for his podcasts.

The results?

▸ Approximately 300 to 1,100 people download each of Ehret's podcasts within four weeks of the new segments becoming available.

▸ Ehret's website receives approximately 17 percent of its traffic from referring sites, with Twitter in the No. 1 spot until recently.

▸ Although Ehret did not share the specific percentage, he did indicate that Facebook temporarily claimed the No. 1 referral spot from

Twitter just recently. However, both Twitter and Facebook are very close to one another in the amount of traffic they refer to his site.

▸ Although he would not disclose revenues or the number of projects, he did confirm that The Marketing Spot has received project requests from podcast listeners.

Ehret summarized his experience with social networking by sharing the following. "Stephen, I believe that every small business owner must participate in social networking in today's business environment. In fact, I think participation in social networking is essential to being successful. This new medium, unlike any other, has given me the ability to share my experience with clients and prospects, demonstrate my credibility, and become a recognized authority among my expanding group of listeners. I definitely plan to continue using social networking and building my online community."

Success story No. 3: William Carr, founder of AutismLyrics.com

William Carr is the founder of AutismLyrics.com, which serves as an online collection of autism songs and lyrics about autism. Carr is passionate about finding a cure for autism because one in 91 American children is afflicted with the disease. While there is no cure, over the past decade, significant strides have been made to improve the treatment options for children on the autism spectrum. Carr has used AutismLyrics.com to help spread awareness of autism through music.

All of the autism songs in this collection are carefully reviewed by hand-selected editors, songwriters, music producers, and media professionals for quality and accuracy. Music therapy for autism is an important element for the company because these autism songs can improve the communication skills in children with autism spectrum disorder (ASD).

Most of the songs featured within the website are available for purchase on iTunes®, Amazon, Napster®, and other MP3 retailers. Some of the autism songs give all or a portion of its proceeds to various autism awareness foundations.

Carr has effectively used Facebook to promote the availability of new songs and lyrics. In fact, he uses both a business Facebook profile and his personal Facebook profile to announce new developments at AutismLyrics.com.

Carr has been pleased with the amount of traffic that has been referred to his website via Facebook. He has considered incorporating Twitter and LinkedIn into his social networking strategy, but so far, he has not invested the time toward blending these audiences into the overall mix.

Carr ingeniously used Facebook to increase the number of in-bound links pointing back to his website. For example, he created a voting poll on his website where he asked visitors to vote for their favorite songs from a list Carr provided. He announced the availability of the poll via his Facebook profiles. He then e-mailed all of his artists the links to the results pages. The artists in turn distributed Carr's links to all of their social networking community members. Some of the recipients began posting information about the poll results and/or sharing it further within their own communities. The result was a viral distribution of Carr's information across the Internet. All of the forwarding generated additional in-bound links for AutismLyrics.com and contributed to the nearly immediate number of Facebook fans.

The results?

▸ Traffic from his Facebook friends represents approximately 25 percent of the total monthly traffic to AutismLyrics.com.

▸ More than 1,500 people nearly immediately "Liked" his business's Facebook page thanks to Carr's poll project.

▸ Despite the following that his Facebook fan page has received, Carr has noticed that his personal Facebook profile still refers more traffic to AutismLyrics.com.

Carr summarized his experience with social networking by sharing the following. "Stephen, I think the main reason my personal Facebook profile has been more successful than our business's Facebook page at referring traffic to AutismLyrics.com is because of the personal relationship I have with my Facebook friends. People within my personal community know me, what I represent, and the principles I stand for. At times, I think the Facebook business pages are a bit impersonal. But regardless, participation in Facebook has been a terrific tool for helping us spread Autism awareness."

CONCLUSION

Thank you for taking time to read and study my viral social networking process. I suspect you began experimenting with many of the steps in the book while reading. If so, my hope is that you received the results you needed in order to find the encouragement and confidence to finish the complete 15 steps.

I think this is an appropriate spot in the book to share one final comment. One of the aspects that make this social networking process so powerful is not found in any of the individual steps themselves. Part of the power of the process is the full process itself. For example, successfully implementing Step 5 gives you the foundation you need to be successful in Step 6, 7, 8, and so on. You will experience the greatest results by implementing the full process because the steps are interconnected with one another.

To quickly reiterate the offer I made at the beginning of the last chapter, I am in search of small business owners who have experience blending search engine optimization with social networking, e-mail marketing, content development, pay-per-click advertising, and more. Please drop me a line if you are willing to share your story. You can reach me at info@ seotrainingproducts.com. I look forward to hearing from you, and I wish you the best of success!

Resources and Suggested Reading

- *Twitter Tips, Tricks, and Tweets* by Paul McFedries

- *The 4-Hour Workweek* by Timothy Ferriss

- *The Constant Contact Guide to Email Marketing* by Eric Groves

- Constant Contact (**www.constantcontact.com**)

- NutshellMail (**http://nutshellmail.com**)

- SEOTrainingProducts.com (**http://seotrainingproducts.com**)

- Bad Axe Tool Works (**www.badaxetoolworks.com**)

- Catherine Tryon Consulting (**www.catherinetryon.com**)

- Dessert Gallery (**www.dessertgallery.com**)

- Google Analytics (**www.google.com/analytics**)

- comScore (**www.comscore.com/Press_Events/Presentations_ Whitepapers/2010/The_2009_U.S._Digital_Year_in_Review**)

- Quantcast (**www.quantcast.com/twitter.com/ demographics#summary**)

- LinkedIn Marketing Solutions (**http://advertising.linkedin.com/audience**)

- Bernadot Studios (**http://bernadot.com**)

- Stein Counseling & Consulting Services (**https://effectivebehavior.com**)

- Bad Axe Tool Works (**www.badaxetoolworks.com/ bad-axe-tool-works-facebook.html**)

- Facebook Brand Permissions Center (**www.facebook.com/ brandpermissions/**)

- Guidelines for Use of the Twitter Trademark (**http://help.twitter. com/entries/77641**)

- LinkedIn Logo Use and Download (**www.linkedin.com/ static?key=branding**)

- Leading Authorities (**www.leadingauthorities.com**)

- The Association of Small Business Development Centers (**www.asbdc-us.org**)

- ProfNet (**www.profnet.com**)

G L O S S A R Y

The following glossary of social networking-related terms was reprinted with permission of Aaron Wall, owner of SEOBook.com, as well as Paul McFedries, author of *Twitter Tips, Tricks, and Tweets*.

AdWords

Google's advertisement and link-auction network. Most of Google's ads are keyword targeted and sold on a cost-per-click basis in an auction, which factors in ad click-through rate, as well as max bid. Google is looking into expanding its ad network to include video ads, demographic targeting, affiliate ads, radio ads, and traditional print ads. AdWords is an increasingly complex marketplace. One could write a 300-page book just covering AdWords.

Analytics

Software that allows you to track your page views, user paths, and conversion statistics based on interpreting your log files or through including a JavaScript tracking code on your site. Ad networks are a game of margins. Marketers who track user action will have a distinct advantage over those who do not.

See also:

> ▸ **Google Analytics**: Google's free analytics program.
> ▸ **ConversionRuler:** A simple, cheap Web-based analytic tool.
> ▸ **ClickTracks:** Downloadable, Web-based analytics software.

Anchor text

The text a user would click on to follow a link. If the link is an image, the image's alt text can act in the place of anchor text.

Search engines assume that your page is authoritative for the words that people include in links pointing at your site. When links occur naturally, they have a wide array of anchor text combinations. Too much similar anchor text may be considered a sign of manipulation and, thus, discounted or filtered. Make sure when you are building links that you control and try to mix up your anchor text.

Example of anchor text: <a href="http://www.seobook.com/">Search Engine Optimization Blog</a>

Outside of your core brand terms, if you are targeting Google, you probably do not want any more than 10 to 20 percent of your anchor text to be the same. You can use Backlink Analyzer to compare the anchor text profile of other top-ranked competing sites.

See also:

> ▸ **Backlink Analyzer (http://tools.seobook.com/backlink-analyzer/):** A free tool to analyze your link anchor text.

Avatar

The user icon associated with a Twitter account.

Badge

A small graphic with a Twitter-inspired design that you use as a link to your Twitter home page.

Blog

A periodically updated journal on the Internet, typically formatted in reverse chronological order. Many blogs not only archive and categorize information but also provide a feed and allow simple user interaction like leaving comments on the posts.

Most blogs tend to be personal in nature. Blogs are quite authoritative with heavy site popularity because they give people a reason to frequently come back to the site, read the blog's content, and link to whatever they think is interesting. The most popular blogging platforms are WordPress, Blogger, Movable Type, and TypePad.

Blogger

Blogger is a free blog platform owned by Google. It allows you to publish sites on a subdomain of Blogspot.com or to file transfer protocol (FTP) content to your own domain. If you are serious about building a brand or making money online, you should publish your content to your own domain because it can be hard to reclaim a website's link equity and age-related trust if you have built years of link equity into a subdomain on someone else's website. Blogger is probably the easiest blogging software tool to use, but it lacks some features present in other blog platforms.

Bot

An automated Twitter account that returns some kind of data in response to a specially formatted message.

Celebritweet

A celebrity or famous person who uses Twitter.

Content Management System (CMS)

A tool used to help make it easy to update and add information to a website. Blog software programs are some of the most popular content management systems currently used on the Web. Many content management systems have errors associated with them, which makes it hard for search engines to index content because of issues like duplicate content.

Conversion

Many forms of online advertising are easy to track. A conversion is reached when a desired goal is completed. Most offline ads have been much harder to track than online ads. Some marketers use custom phone numbers or coupon codes to tie offline activity to online marketing. Here are a few common examples of desired goals:

- A product sale
- Completing a lead form
- A phone call
- Capturing an e-mail
- Filling out a survey
- Getting a person to pay attention to you
- Getting feedback
- Having a site visitor share your website with a friend
- Having a site visitor link to your site

Bid management, affiliate tracking, and analytics programs make it easy to track conversion sources

See also:

- ▸ **Google Conversion University:** Free conversion tracking information.
- ▸ **Google Website Optimizer:** Free multivariable testing product offered by Google.

CSS

Cascading Style Sheets add styles to Web documents. Note: Using external CSS files makes it easy to change the design of many pages by editing a single file. You can link to an external CSS file using a code similar to the following in the head of your HTML documents:

<link rel="stylesheet" href="http://www.seobook.com/style.css" type="text/css" />.

See also:

- ▸ **W3C (www.w3.org):** Official guidelines for CSS.
- ▸ **CSS Zen Garden (www.csszengarden.com):** Examples of various CSS layouts.
- ▸ **Glish.com:** Examples of various CSS layouts and links to other CSS resources.

Click-through rate (CTR)

The percentage of people who click on an advertisement they viewed. This is a way to measure how relevant a traffic source or keyword is. Search ads normally have a higher click-through rate than traditional banner ads because of being highly relevant to implied searcher demand.

Digg

Social news site (**http://digg.com**) where users vote on which stories get the most exposure and become the most popular.

Direct

To send a direct message to someone; a direct message.

Direct message

A private note on Twitter that only the recipient can read.

Domain

Scheme used for logical or location organization of the Web. Many people also use the word domain to refer to a specific website.

Dreamweaver

Popular Web development and editing software offering a what-you-see-is-what-you-get interface.

Entry page

The page on which a user enters your site. If you are buying pay-per-click ads, it is important to send visitors to the most appropriate and targeted page associated with the keyword they searched for. If you are doing link building, it is important to point links at your most appropriate page when possible so that when someone clicks the link, they are taken to the most appropriate and relevant page.

Exactotweet

See twoosh.

Fail whale

The page that Twitter displays when it is over capacity and cannot accept any more Tweets.

Feed

Many content management systems, such as blogs, allow readers to subscribe to content update notifications via RSS or XML feeds. Feeds can also refer to pay-per-click syndicated feeds or merchant product feeds. Merchant product feeds have become less effective as a means of content generation because of improving duplicate content filters.

Feed reader

Software or website used to subscribe to feed update notifications.

See also:

- **Bloglines:** Popular Web-based feed reader.
- **Google Reader:** Popular Web-based feed reader.
- **My Yahoo!:** Allows you to subscribe to feed updates.
- **FeedDemon:** Desktop-based feed reader.

Flash

Vector graphics-based animation software, which makes it easier to make websites look rich and interactive in nature. Search engines tend to struggle indexing and ranking flash websites because flash contains so little relevant content. If you use flash, ensure:

- You embed flash files within HTML pages.
- You use a no-embed element to describe what is in the flash.
- You publish your flash content in multiple separate files such that you can embed appropriate flash files in relevant pages.

Followership

The people who follow a particular Twitter user.

Followorthy

Worthy of being followed on Twitter.

Hashtag

A word that, when preceded by a hash (#), defines or references a topic on Twitter.

Home page

The main page on your website, which is largely responsible for helping develop your brand and setting up the navigational schemes that will be used to help users and search engines navigate your website. As far as SEO goes, a home page is going to be one of the easier pages to rank for some of your more competitive terms, largely because it is easy to build links at a home page. You should ensure your home page stays focused and reinforces your brand though, and do not assume that most of your visitors will come to your site via the home page. If your site is well structured, many pages on your site will likely be far more popular and rank better than your home page for relevant queries.

Hypertweeting

Posting an excessive number of Tweets.

Information architecture

Designing, categorizing, organizing, and structuring content in a useful, meaningful way. Good information architecture considers how both humans and search engine spiders access a website. Information architecture suggestions:

- Focus each page on a specific topic.
- Use descriptive page titles and meta descriptions that describe the content of the page.
- Use clean — few or no variables — descriptive file names and folder names.
- Use headings to help break up text and semantically structure a document.
- Use breadcrumb navigation to show page relationships.
- Use descriptive link anchor text.
- Link to related information from within the content area of your Web pages.
- Improve conversion rates by making it easy for people to take desired actions.
- Avoid feeding search engines duplicate or near-duplicate content.

Landing Page

The page on which a visitor arrives after clicking on a link or advertisement.

Link

A citation from one Web document to another or to another position in the same document. Most major search engines consider links as a vote of trust.

Link Building

The process of building high-quality linkage data that search engines will evaluate to trust your website is authoritative, relevant, and trustworthy. A few general link-building tips:

- Build conceptually unique, link-worthy, high-quality content.
- Create viral marketing ideas that want to spread and make people talk about you.

- ▸ Mix your anchor text.

- ▸ Get deep links.

- ▸ Try to build at least a few quality links before actively obtaining any low-quality links.

- ▸ Register your site in relevant high-quality directories, such as DMOZ, the Yahoo! Directory, and Business.com.

- ▸ When possible, try to focus your efforts mainly on getting high-quality editorial links.

- ▸ Create link bait.

- ▸ Try to get bloggers to mention you on their blogs.

- ▸ It takes a while to catch up with the competition, but if you work at it long enough and hard enough, eventually, you can enjoy a self-reinforcing market position.

Link popularity

The number of links pointing to a website. For competitive search queries, link quality counts much more than link quantity. Google shows a smaller sample of known linkage data than the other engines do, even though Google still counts many of the links they do not show when you do a link search.

Live-tweeting

Sending on-the-fly updates that describe or summarize some ongoing event.

Log files

Server files, which show you what your leading sources of traffic are and what people are searching for to find your website. Log files do not show as much data as analytics programs would, and if they do, it is not in a format that is as useful beyond seeing the top few stats.

Mashup

Information created by combining data from two or more different sources.

Meme

A cultural artifact, such as an idea or catchphrase, that spreads quickly from person to person.

Micro-blogging

Posting short thoughts and ideas to an online site, such as Twitter.

Mutual follow

When two people on Twitter follow each other.

Navigation

Scheme to help website users understand where they are, where they have been, and how that relates to the rest of your website. It is best to use regular HTML navigation rather than coding your navigation in JavaScript, Flash, or some other type of navigation that search engines might not be able to index easily.

Nudge

A text message sent to your phone to remind you to post an update.

Partial Retweet

A Retweet that includes only part of the original Tweet.

Reciprocal Links

Nepotistic link exchanges where websites try to build false authority by trading links, using three-way link trades, or using other low-quality link schemes. When sites link naturally, there is going to be some amount of cross-linking within a community, but if most or all of your links are reciprocal in nature, it may be a sign of ranking manipulation. Also, sites that trade links off topic or on links pages that are stashed away deep within their sites probably do not pass much link authority and may add more risk than reward.

Quality reciprocal link exchanges in and of themselves are not a bad thing, but most reciprocal link offers are of low quality. If too many of your links are of low quality, it might make it harder for your site to rank for relevant queries, and some search engines might look at inlink and outlink ratios, as well as link quality, when determining how natural a site's link profile is.

Referrer

The source from which a website visitor came.

Reply

A response to a Tweeter's update.

Retweet

Another person's Tweet that you copy and send out to your followers, along with an acknowledgement of the original Tweeter.

Return on investment (ROI)

A measure of how much return you receive from each marketing dollar. Although ROI is a somewhat sophisticated measurement, some search marketers prefer to account for their marketing using more sophisticate profit elasticity calculations.

RT

An abbreviation used to mark an update as a Retweet; a Retweet.

Search engine optimization (SEO)

The art and science of publishing information and marketing it in a manner that helps search engines understand your information is relevant to specific search queries. SEO consists largely of keyword research, SEO copywriting, information architecture, link building, brand building, building mindshare, reputation management, and viral marketing.

Spam

Unsolicited e-mail messages. Search engines also like to outsource their relevancy issues by calling low-quality search results spam. They have vague, ever-changing guidelines, which determine what marketing techniques are acceptable at any given time. Normally, search engines try hard not to flag false positives as spam so most algorithms are quite lenient, as long as you do not build many low-quality links, host large quantities of duplicate content, or perform other actions considered widely outside of relevancy guidelines. If your site is banned from a search engine, you can request re-inclusion after fixing the problem.

Text link ads

Advertisements formatted as text links. Because the Web was originally based on text and links, people are more inclined to pay attention to text links than some other ad formats, which are less relevant and more annoying. However, search engines primarily want to count editorial links as votes so links that are grouped together with other paid links — especially if those links are to off-topic commercial sites — might be less likely to carry weight in search engines.

Timeline

A related collection of Tweets, sorted by the date and time they were posted.

Tweeple

People who use Twitter.

Tweeps

A Twitter user's friends.

Tweet

An update posted to Twitter.

Tweet cred

Twitter credibility.

Tweeter

A person who uses Twitter.

Tweetstream

The Tweets in a timeline.

Tweetup

A real-world meeting between two or more people who know each other through the online Twitter service.

Tweetwalking

Writing and posting a Twitter update while walking.

Tweme

A twitter meme.

Twittaholic

A person who uses Twitter compulsively.

Twitterati

The Twitter users with the most followers and influence.

Twitterpated

Overwhelmed by incoming Tweets.

Twitterverse

The Twitter social networking service and the people who use it.

Twitticism

A witty Tweet.

Twittiquette

Twitter etiquette; an informal set of guidelines and suggestions for updating, following, replying, and sending direct messages.

Twoosh

A Tweet exactly 140 characters long.

Tword

A new word created by appending "tw" to an existing word.

URL

Uniform Resource Locator is the unique address of any Web document.

URL shortening service

A website or program that converts a Web address into a much shorter URL and then uses that URL to redirect users to the original address.

Viral marketing

Self-propagating marketing techniques. Common modes of transmission are e-mail, blogging, and word-of-mouth marketing channels. Many social news sites and social bookmarking sites also lead to secondary citations.

Wiki

Software that allows information to be published using collaborative editing.

Wikipedia

Free online collaborative encyclopedia using wiki software. See also: **Wikipedia.org**.

WordPress

A popular, open-source blogging software platform, offering both a downloadable blogging program and a hosted solution. If you are serious about building a brand or making money online, you should publish your content to your own domain because it can be hard to reclaim a website's link equity and age-related trust if you have built years of link equity into a subdomain on someone else's website.

See also:

- **WordPress.org:** Download the software.
- **WordPress.com:** Offers free blog hosting.

BIBLIOGRAPHY

Anonymous. (2009, March.) "Papa John's Finds New Facebook Fans by Dangling Free Pizza." *Brandweek*, 50 (10), 6.

Betts, M. (2009, June 22.) "Tweet Deals." *Computerworld*, 43 (22), 31-31.

Corbett, P. (2010, January 4) "Facebook Demographics and Statistics Report 2010 – 145% Growth in 1 Year." *iStrategyLabs* (2011, January 11.) <**http://www.istrategylabs.com/2010/01/facebook-demographics-and-statistics-report-2010-145-growth-in-1-year/**>.

De Bruyn, A., & Lilien, G. (2008.) "A multi-stage model of word-of-mouth influence through viral marketing." *International Journal of Research in Marketing*, 25, 151-163.

Dholakia, U. M. and Durham, E. (2010, March.) "One Café Chain's Facebook Experiment." *Harvard Business Review*, < **http://hbr. org/2010/03/one-cafe-chains-facebook-experiment/ar/1**>.

Dholakia, U.M., Bagozzi, R.P., & Pearo, L.K. (2004.) "A Social Influence Model of Consumer Participation in Network- and Small-Group-Based Virtual Communities." *International Journal of Research in Marketing*, 21, 241-264.

"Facebook." Wikipedia. (2011, January 11.) <**http://en.wikipedia.org/ wiki/Facebook**>.

Gaudin, S. (2010, January 26.) "Twitter now has 75M users; most asleep at the mouse." *Computerworld Magazine*. <**http://www.computerworld.com/s/article/9148878/ Twitter_now_has_75M_users_most_asleep_at_the_mouse**>.

Gaudin, S. (2009, March 16.) "Web 2.0 Tools Can Foster Growth in Hard Times." *Computerworld*, 43 (11), 12-14.

Klaassen, A. (2009, May 18.) "Twitter Proves Its Worth as a Killer App for Local Businesses." *Advertising Age*, 80 (18), 32-32.

Sen, S., & Lerman, D. (2007.) "Why are you telling me this? An examination into negative consumer reviews on the Web." *Journal of Interactive Marketing*, 21 (4), 76-94.

Thompson, S., & Sinha, R. (2008.) "Brand Communities and New Product Adoption: The Influence and Limits of Oppositional Loyalty." *Journal of Marketing*, 72 (6), 65-80.

AUTHOR

Stephen Woessner

Stephen Woessner has 17 years of experience in Web strategy development, social networking, search engine optimization, e-commerce, e-mail marketing, and strategic planning. He has had the privilege of consulting with hundreds of clients on the development of websites and online marketing strategies. In 2006, Woessner decided to leave private sector consulting and accepted a position at the University of Wisconsin-La Crosse Small Business Development Center (SBDC). He is an SBDC business adviser, instructor, author, and a frequent speaker.

Woessner also understand the day-to-day pressures and challenges of running a business because he has owned four of his own, including SEOTrainingProducts.com.

Inc. Magazine, E-commerce Times, B-to-B Online Magazine, The Milwaukee Journal-Sentinel, Wisconsin Public Radio, and other media have interviewed Woessner regarding various online marketing topics. He teaches search engine optimization and social networking classes at the University of Wisconsin-Madison, UW-La Crosse, UW-Green Bay, UW-Superior, UW-Parkside, and Kent State University-Stark. The classes are practical and tactical in nature and are attended by business owners and managers.

In addition to this book, Woessner also wrote *The Small Business Owner's Handbook to Search Engine Optimization,* which has been the No. 3 best-selling book on Amazon.com United States, No. 1 on Amazon.com United Kingdom, and No. 16 on Amazon.com France for its category. His first book was also published by Atlantic Publishing Group, Inc. (**www.atlantic-pub.com**). You can find Woessner on Facebook, LinkedIn, Twitter, or Google.

INDEX

Also by Stephen Woessner

The Small Business Owner's Handbook to Search Engine Optimization: Increase Your Google Rankings, Double Your Site Traffic ... In Just 15 Steps - Guaranteed

The Small Business Owner's Handbook to Search Engine Optimization is ideal for small business owners who want to learn an efficient and effective process for dramatically improving their website's search engine rankings and doubling their site's monthly unique visitors. Guaranteed! Stephen Woessner, of the University of Wisconsin-La Crosse's Small Business Development Center, is a search engine optimization (SEO) expert. But more importantly, Woessner has owned four businesses and understands the significant time and cash constraints faced by business owners every day. Because of this, Woessner placed increasing efficiency and effectiveness at the core of the 15 steps, allowing a business owner to maximize results in as little time as possible. A business owner does not need to know technical skills, like Web programming, to be successful at SEO. Instead, business owners will rely on their marketing skills and the ability to think like their customers and prospects, versus an ability to write HTML or other form of Web programming. Business owners will learn how to select keywords that are proven performers, blend the keywords into site content, boost site popularity, and more. Woessner explains with precision how business owners can use SEO to achieve measurable results. This practical and tactical guide includes a free SEO toolkit and other valuable resources that will help business owners increase the returnon investment generated by their websites. Business owners will also receive a detailed blueprint with specific checklists to follow throughout the 15-step process. Lastly, this book can also serve as an excellent resource to business owners who are considering outsourcing their SEO work to a third party. Developing a working knowledge of the 15-step process will make any business owner a more informed consumer. This book is also an ideal resource for marketing and advertising agency professionals who want to expand their services and need to develop a proficiency in SEO as efficiently and effectively as possible.

ISBN-13: 978-1-60138-443-0 • $24.95
288 Pgs • $24.95 • 2009 RELEASE